THE COMPLETE
KARATE
HANDBOOK

THE COMPLETE
KARATE
HANDBOOK

FRANK T. PERRY
WITH DESMOND MARWOOD

WARD LOCK

First published in Great Britain in 1990
by Ward Lock, Villiers House, 41/47 Strand, London WC2N 5JE

A Cassell company

Photography by Gerald Place

British Library Cataloguing in Publication Data
Perry, Frank
  The Karate handbook.
  1. Karate
  I. Title II. Marwood, Desmond
  796.8153
  ISBN 0-7063-6902-5

Typeset by August Filmsetting, Haydock, St Helens
Printed in Britain by Bath Press

Contents

Acknowledgements and useful Addresses

For the provision of equipment photographed in this book, grateful thanks to Meijin Martial Arts Supplies, 141, Goldhawk Road, London W12, and to Tokaido of Japan.

The Author and Publishers would like to thank Kumiko-Bartlett for the provision of Japanese Gyosho script and Sensei Chris Mansfield (Kendo) who helped with its editorial preparation.

For any information about Karate, write directly to the English Karate Council, the British Karate Federation, or the Martial Arts Commission, who are all available at 1st Floor, Broadway House, 15–16, Deptford Broadway, London SE8 4PE.

For regional purposes, others may need to contact the European Karate Union, 122, Rue de la Tombe Issoire, 75014 Paris, France.

Enquiries from North American students should be sent to Mr George Anderson, WUKO Representative USA, at 1300, Kenmore Boulevard, Akron, Ohio 44314, United States of America.

Enquiries to the World Union of Karate Organizations should be addressed to Mr N. Yomoaka, General Secretary WUKO, Senpaku Shinko Bldg, 1/15/16 Tordunomon, Minato-Ku, Tokyo 105, Japan.

Foreword

Karate is one of today's fastest growing leisure-time activities. Adult and child students of both sexes are attracted by the enhancement of harmony between mind and body and the ensuing improvement in individual fitness that Karate offers. There are also, of course, the self-defence benefits of Karate and the confidence it provides. Such confidence is particularly beneficial to women who must cope with today's sometimes undisciplined and dangerous society. For any student with a competitive spirit, there is the enjoyment to be derived from taking part in competitive Karate, which is a highly organized sport.

The popular appeal of these combined elements is the result of sustained and dedicated work from those who have practised and pioneered Karate since its introduction by the Japanese Masters. Frank Perry is one of those *karate-ka* who have worked to promote and maintain the true standards of *karate-do*, whilst at the same time fostering *bushido*. He successfully made the transition from being a top competitor to being a leading administrator with the English Karate Council. He has taken an active role in the organization of coaching courses for Karate instructors, to ensure not only that the public receives the most skilled and proficient instruction, but also that full adherence to safety standards is observed.

Karate

I am pleased that all these aspects of Karate are referred to in this book, and that the importance for the beginner of becoming a student member of a group which is properly recognized by or registered with the Martial Arts Commission, is stressed. This basic and common-sense advice accompanies the true traditional spirit of *karate-do* in this book, making it an invaluable source of inspiration as well as reference for all who practise Karate.

Barney Whelan
Chairman,
Martial Arts Commission

About the Author

Frank Perry is 6th Dan Kyoshi and holds Dan grade levels in Judo, Aikido, Kendo, Kobudo and Jujutsu. As a Karate Master, he runs the largest full-time Karate *dojo* in England and his school, the United Kingdom *Seiku-Juku* Karate Organization, has thousands of registered students.

Frank Perry worked originally with the first Japanese Budo and Karate exponents who came to Britain. From the former, he acquired what is now a rare knowledge of the Bushido Spirit (the martial way of the classical warrior) and this remains something he wishes to see fostered today in all Martial Arts.

As a competitor, Frank Perry has fought at national and international level and his students have won numerous honours. He has devoted much time and energy to the establishment of Karate as a fast-growing sport with behind-the-scenes work on the English Karate Council, of which he became Vice-Chairman in 1988. He is also Chairman of the English Karate Council Technical and Coaching Committees and is the English representative to the British Karate Federation. Other appointments include that of Chief Instructor of the United Kingdom *Seiku-Juku* Karate Organization and also of the *Koku Sai-Budo-Shingi Kai.*

Frank Perry has presented Martial Art techniques for television and was also the subject of the first ever documentary Karate film distributed nationwide in cinemas. This film demonstrated, among other Karate techniques, the build-up to his successful breaking of a stack of nine huge ice blocks with a single hand strike in a display of *tameshiwari* never seen on screen before.

Introduction

In 1957, when I was only four years old, my elder brother took me along to see what went on at our local Martial Arts school where *Sensei* Kaoru Mishiku taught Judo, Ken-jutsu and Ju-jutsu. At first, my brother and other students regarded me as no more than their 'mascot', but what had started out as a joke soon became quite a serious business. For, despite my age, I established an almost immediate rapport and understanding with the *sensei* (teacher). I was accepted by him as a regular pupil and continued to study with him during the many years that followed.

Sensei Kaoru Mishiku was Japanese and of true Samurai stock. He had come to London from Japan in 1909 and he remained until his death. Around the early sixties, the first of the Karate Masters from Japan arrived in London, some at the invitation of *Sensei* Kaoru Mishiku. So, at the age of fourteen, I found myself taking up Karate as a natural follow-on to the other disciplines I had studied, and continue to study today.

In fact, my whole life has been centred around and consumed by the study of Martial Arts and of Karate in particular. I can only assume that having taken up Martial Arts at such a tender age explains why I now regarded **doing** Karate and **enjoying** Karate as a normal way of life. Karate has taken me all round the world as a Martial Arts student, instructor, coach, competitor and simply as one in pursuit of personal knowledge about Karate and its roots. The physical and spiritual rewards have been limitless and I have enjoyed the meeting and exchange of respects with many great people.

, However, I shall always regard myself fortunate to have been living in London during the formative years of Karate in the UK. Then, during the 1960s and early 1970s, there was an abundance of Japanese Martial Arts Masters living and teaching in the city. That made it possible to study Karate under any one of a number of Japanese Masters, who were all highly qualified teachers from traditional backgrounds. These ethnic tutors would be prepared to spend years teaching a small group of selected students, and to each they gave maximum attention. As much time was devoted to sound character training and the whole *karate-do* (philosophy) which goes into the make-up of the complete *karate-ka* (one who studies Karate), as was to the physical side of things. For, in Karate, both physical and mental attitudes are, or should be, inseparable.

Such an approach to Karate and its teaching may appear in stark contrast to the contemporary approach, with its large schools and institutions, bureaucratic associations and massive sports halls in which

Karate is taught alongside basketball, tennis, gymnastics, and other sports.

On the other hand, the improvement in Karate as a competitive sport since it was introduced as such into the UK in 1967 has been dramatic. It may be that the administration of Karate as a fast-growing sporting event requires such impersonal facilities and supporting bodies to control its organization. Certainly, in sporting terms, it is difficult to challenge the broad aspects of Karate's sporting structure when looking at the end results. United Kingdom Karate is now recognized to be the finest in the world and we have contributed much to the global development of the sport. Indeed, the UK team has won the World Championship four times – more than any other nation, including Japan.

However, only a few of those who take up Karate ever aspire to, let alone become capable of, achieving championship status of any sort. Most don't look for any kind of contest work beyond that which may be demanded of them at various stages of grading examinations. So, what sort of person takes up Karate?

At my own club, Bu'sen, we have males and females, schoolchildren, students, doctors, architects, solicitors, tradesmen, people from right across the social spectrum. We have mums and dads and even whole families. A plain white karate *gi* (karate suit) is a great social leveller, and status in the outside commercial world provides no automatic passport to a *dojo* (translated, this means a place of practice or enlightenment), nor does it guarantee respect from instructors or fellow students. Neither is physical perfection a necessary requisite. Karate can even provide stimulation for some afflicted with handicaps such as certain learning difficulties or problems of reaction. Deafness, also, is certainly no disqualification.

The follow-up question is: why do people take up Karate? The 'why' is a far more difficult and complex question to answer than the 'who'. Some, particularly the very young, may be easily attracted by the popular image of Karate as portrayed so dramatically by the media. Others may simply be in search of physical fitness, in which case they might just as easily take up weight training. For those attracted by the competitive aspect of a fighting sport there is always boxing. Those wishing to acquire self-defence and counter-attack skills against street muggers could join any one of the many classes being run for this purpose.

It is my opinion that there is never one single reason why people take up Karate. It does engender a respect and discipline which is easily recognizable and these qualities in themselves attract many beginners. The real rewards, however, come later.

Providing that initial interest and enthusiasm survive beyond a beginner's course, most individuals then go on to discover the special qualities of Karate. It becomes something to be enjoyed and looked forward to; something at which the individual can from the outset begin to excel within his or her own range of capabilities, however modest they may be. Thereafter, the individual's driving force to further progress is the constant challenge of self-improvement, of harmonious reaction

Sensei Frank T. Perry

between mind and body. The body's reactions to messages from the brain begin to quicken, eventually happening so quickly that the individual may not even recall having thought about the action beforehand. Hence, the individual comes towards the discovery of *karate-do* (the karate way).

There are many *do's* in the Japanese language, such as *Ju-do* or *Aiki-do*. In fact both the Tea Ceremony and Flower Arranging are considered to be 'ways'. Any discipline requiring a special effort is called a *do* (or way). *Karate-do*, therefore, is a way which demands of the *karate-ka* a dedicated and concentrated struggle with the inner person for self-improvement in all things and in all aspects of life in or out of the *dojo*. The aim is to maximize working harmony between mind and body in all things.

This is reflected in my own school, the United Kingdom *Seiki-Juku* Karate Organization. *Seiki-Juku* means 'True Spirit' and our *mon* (badge) shows an English rose amongst three circles representing Purity, Diligence and Respect.

The word *karate* itself means 'empty hand', one incapable of grasping or holding on to pride, prejudice or any other selfish desire. The empty hand is to be offered to others in the service of life itself.

All this is a simplistic outline of the *karate-do* philosophy which is far from being confined, one way or another, to any single school. Its principles should be cornerstones to the mentality of any *karate-ka*. Though few are able to discuss the philosophy of Karate in any intellectual depth, many come to experience the existence of its principles and application in an everyday practical sense. This is the ultimate reward for years of dedication and hard work. Such a marriage between spirit and body in all students is, or should be, aimed for by any good Karate *sensei* in order to bring out the highest mental and physical standards in every individual. This should not only improve the *dojo* performance of every *karate-ka*, but also help make each of them a more caring and better-equipped member of society.

My hope is that this book will stimulate the beginner to start out in the right direction, to work hard and perfect all his or her all-round abilities as a *karate-ka*.

The History of Karate

Much has been spoken and written about the history of Karate and the origins of the Chinese Martial Arts from which it is believed to have evolved. However, little or no documentation is ever produced to support any historian's version of how it all began, each recorder usually choosing to recount a tale which best suits the background of their own particular style or school of Karate.

In fact, there is no documented evidence to prove that Martial Arts, as perceived or practised today, existed in China before the coming of one *Bodhidharma* around the year AD 520. He was an Indian who had travelled to China, where he is reported to have spent nine years in meditation at the Buddhist Shao Lin Temple.

During that period, he devoted some of his meditations to the creation of a Martial Art form which could be used by the monks who were often called upon to defend the monastery against marauding bandits who roamed and plundered the countryside. The practice of this new form of fighting, or Martial Art, both increased the monks' physical strengths, and subjected them to meditation training through which they developed greater powers of endurance. So, at least some of the origins of that which later became called Karate, are to be found rooted in the Buddhism of China.

My belief is that the true development of what we call Karate may be attributed to the people of the Okinawan Islands and this may be endorsed by examining their history.

The Okinawan Masters

In 1340, Okinawa was divided into three kingdoms. They became known as the Okinawa Ryukyu Islands Dynasty and as such established a relationship with China. Arising from this association, various types of delegates and skilled craftsmen were sent to Okinawa from China. Many of the Chinese visitors brought with them their own Martial Arts skills.

Then, around the 1470s, came the collapse of Okinawa's *Sho* Dynasty which was followed by a period of political unrest. Eventually, a new Dynasty was established; and to help restore law and order in Okinawa, a ban was placed throughout the land upon the carrying of swords by either nobleman or peasant. All the nobility were invited to live within the Royal capital where the authorities were able to keep an eye on their warlords to ensure they remained unarmed and well behaved. It was partly because of this ban upon the carrying of swords that Okinawans turned to the 'open hand' and other methods of attack and defence, including the use of agricultural implements as weapons.

Although there was at that time no such word as Karate designated to any Martial Art form, there emerged in Okinawan records dated 1756 the first mention of any recognized Masters of these new fighting skills – a Master Wansu and another Master, Kusanku. These early masters provide another link with today's Karate, as two *kata* are still named after them (see reference to them later in *The Importance of Kata*).

It was not until the early part of the twentieth century that Karate became the recognized Japanese name of Okinawa's particular form of Martial Art. Thereafter, various Karate styles began taking on individual names instead of being *te* or *todei*, meaning 'hand' or 'Chinese hand' respectively.

By then, many of the Shaolin and Boxer peoples had been forced to leave China following the Boxer rebellion and had taken their *wusu* martial art skills with them to islands such as Okinawa, mainland Japan and parts of Malaysia. Amongst this great cross-fertilization of Eastern cultures were the Okinawan Masters, who took their Karate skills to mainland Japan, where its own people had been steeped for centuries in

Bodhidharma, now referred to in Japan as Daruma, depicted as a wooden effigy, its rotund form symbolizing the manner in which he eventually lost the use of his legs after long periods of meditation.

Martial Art forms such as *Ju-jutsu* and *Ken-jutsu*. Schools dedicated to the teaching of these disciplines existed in abundance throughout Japan and this new form called *Karate* was not at first very well received. Karate had to struggle for recognition.

Finally, in 1933, Karate became acknowledged by the Japanese *Butokuwai*, which was then the country's governing body for all of Japan's Martial Arts activities. The Okinawan Masters resident in Japan changed the translation of Karate from 'Chinese hand' to 'empty hand'. This seemed more strongly to signify a change from *jutsu*, or pure fighting technique, into *do*, which presented a more all-round challenging development of human qualities. And so we have *karate-do*.

'Empty' hand also symbolizes the open-mindedness and spirit of the Karate student's attitude. This was, and still is, that the surest way to eventually lose something is to grasp and hold onto it to for too long. This philosophy had meaningful applications in attitudes towards practice and combat as well as in coping with the more tranquil aspects of everyday life. This marriage between the physical and the spiritual aspects of *karate-do* has already been referred to in the introduction.

The first schools

Having established Karate in Japan, the development and spread of their skills throughout Japan was not easy for the Okinawans. Many schools of Karate were formed by Japanese themselves who had trained with Okinawan teachers. Additionally, some Okinawan teachers decided to leave their main school and branched out with their own philosophies and individual training methods. The first four schools formed in this way in Okinawa were *Gojuryu, Shorinryu, Uechieryu* and *Tomari-te-Shorinryu*. There are now hundreds of such schools throughout Japan, each with its individual approach to the philosophy, teaching, training and application of Karate. Three early pioneers who introduced Japanese Karate into the UK during the early sixties were Master Suzuki, Master Kanazawa and Master Harada.

Karate has continually undergone changes, however slightly, from the original Okinawan traditions, and this has been to suit the particular needs of adopting countries. The basic style of Karate, as taught by the early Okinawans, would almost certainly have been adapted to the requirements of mainland Japan. Similarly, the mainstream of Karate in the UK has itself developed to suit European physique and temperament. Despite this, the running theme throughout Karate, whatever the school, contact or non-contact, sporting or not, remains based upon the continuing teaching of a sound physiological science which enables an individual to harness mind and body in harmony to produce explosive but controlled techniques.

All things should be in harmony, yet nothing remains constant. I consider Karate's state of change and development to be desirable. However, I cannot agree with those who have a shallow understanding of Martial Art concepts who make changes for no good reason, or to suit their own limited physical abilities and comprehension.

Karate today

World Karate now has its governing body, the World Union of Karate Organizations (WUKO), which has headquarters in Japan and affiliations in most countries where Karate is practised. There are established sets of rules and regulations for all forms of Karate in sporting competitions.

Whilst the outstanding progress made by Karate as a sporting event is to be applauded, it is important that any further progress made in that direction is not to the detriment of Karate in its widest sense; to the personal development of the *karate-ka*'s all-round individual character and to the practice of *kata* and preservation of our true spirit.

Unless protected by responsible teachers in the main schools, aspects of Karate such as *kata*, self-defence and general character-building of the individual could become secondary to the achievement of sporting honours. This should not be allowed to happen to Karate: every beginner, just as much as the advanced student or even Master, can make a contribution to help retain and foster the full essence of Karate, which is our heritage.

An experienced *karate-ka*'s belt and a well used rope *makawari* shown flanking a *samurai* sword and symbolizing the intrinsic link between the *bushido* spirit (samurai way) and *karate-do*.

Finding Instruction

Junbi

(Preparation/
Exercise)

Once you have decided to take up Karate, for whatever reason, it is probably more important to enquire where to begin rather than how to begin. There are now so many Karate schools and clubs, each of variable styles, qualities and backgrounds, that it's advisable to spend some time shopping around before committing yourself to any of them. Remind yourself that when that point of commitment is reached, it will be the start of a major investment period from you in terms of personal time, dedication and energy. Training is hard and you may expect (this cannot be hidden or ignored!) perhaps your first exhilarating but exhausting experience of passing through pain barriers. You will give, and be expected to give, total dedication to the effort you make in the *dojo*.

All the more important then, that you start off with the right sort of club, one teaching whatever you may consider to be the style of Karate which suits you best, under the tutorship of a properly qualified instructor. You can make a good start by looking for a good instructor or club registered with the Martial Arts Commission, an organization which was set up by the Department of the Environment in 1977 and endorsed as the governing body for all Martial Arts in the UK (apart from Judo which had become recognized as a sport and already had its own official bodies).

This advice is not meant to infer that any instructors outside the MAC are not competent or otherwise qualified, but a lay-member of the public who knows nothing of Karate has no other yardstick by which to assess them. In the past, it has been known for so-called instructors with scant knowledge to hire a hall where they impressed beginner students with a limited range of three or four basic techniques before their 'school' has petered out and died. What a waste of time for those who could so easily have been on the brink of enjoying their Karate.

As a beginner, the problem is to recognize whether or not you are in a proper school of Karate, other than by its registration with the MAC. There are far too many clubs and styles to list and, of course, there's nothing to stop any 'teacher' from forming a club and starting a 'school' named after a recognized style in order to provide some credibility.

Points to look for

From the local church hall Karate class to the biggest Martial Arts centres, you need to be inquisitive before joining. Ask these questions to help determine the good from merely average or downright poor.

● Is the instructor happy to produce his credentials?

● Don't accept that a collection of Japanese names must be authentic – check them out with the MAC or the English Karate Council, which is the governing body for England. Scotland, Wales and Ireland each have their own governing bodies which all come under the British Karate Federation.

● Are the students dressed in a clean and uniform manner?

● Are there categories for beginners, intermediate and advanced students?

● How long has the club been established?

● If the club has been established for some time, is there a reasonable proportion of intermediate or advanced students?

● Is a qualified First Aid person in attendance?

● Do students fight on mats in order to avoid injury from falls?

● Do students wear protective equipment to prevent injury?

● Is the attitude of students towards the teacher one of respect?

● Is the teacher a member of a larger group so that, in his absence, others are able to take over without interfering with training schedules?

● Is the club part of a large group, so that if necessary a student may change clubs and continue training in another area?

Naturally, few clubs would be able to offer favourable replies to all these questions, but acquire a list of clubs in your area from the MAC and canvass them for the one able to offer most.

The MAC will also be able to give some advice about what fees you should be expected to pay for membership, course fees and any other payments you might have to make for special facilities, kit or grading examinations. These do tend to vary.

Most clubs accept juniors from the age of six years and there's no upper age limit right through to the oldest seniors, male and female alike. All students go through a similar syllabus and sequence of grading examinations.

Karate schools

Nowadays, under the rules of the World Union of Karate Organizations, some degree of body contact is allowed by all schools. My own school is concerned with contact Karate as specified in the rules for contests set out by the English Karate Council; that is, opponents striking each other with full force to certain parts of the body. Our training is towards realistic fighting that would serve a student equally well either defending himself in a street fight or competing in a contest.

Sensei Perry preparing to begin a class of senior students with *fudo dachi* (formal stance) prior to exchanging salutations

Conversely, there still remains the occasional non-fighting, non-contact school in which nothing is taught except *kata* (Karate routines) and pre-arranged *kumite* (sparring). Participants are trained to stop a strike fractionally short of contact during one-step practice. Practically all schools teach and practice the skills of *tameshiwari* (the breaking of solid objects) at some time or another and to varying extents.

The different styles of Karate may be considered as many pathways, each winding their own way to the peak of a mountain. Different routes suit various body types and mentalities, as do the different styles of Karate, but all should lead to a similar pinnacle of excellence. This is why the philosophy and basic techniques outlined in this book have been carefully selected for inclusion. They are all used by the varying styles of Karate in one form or another. The physics behind each technique is the same, regardless of school. Beyond that, each student must choose his or her own pathway to the peak.

Preparing for Karate

Shoshin Sha
(Beginner)

The prime requirement for a novice student in Karate is a reasonable level of fitness. Once embarked upon, Karate will certainly keep you fit if practised regularly, but you must be reasonably fit in order to begin. This may pose no problem to the young and active. Older students, who are maybe not even at a level where they could go through a beginner class exercise routine without putting themselves under stress, should consider first taking a supplementary fitness programme as well as a medical check-up with their doctor. At whatever age, a preliminary medical check is always advisable. Even if your doctor gives you clearance to take up Karate, you must inform the *sensei* of your medical condition before commencing training.

For those out of condition for no real medical reason, a forty-five minute brisk daily walk is a good way to begin tuning up. Swimming three or four times a week is an excellent way to attain a standard of pre-Karate class fitness. A mature student will find flexibility one of the hardest goals to achieve and that's one reason why so much importance is placed upon the recommended warming-up exercise routines.

So, having chosen your club and achieved some standard of fitness, all you need now is your *karate-gi* (suit) and you're ready to start.

Karate, contrary to some rumour, is not an expensive activity. A *karate-gi* will probably be obtainable through the club you join. Membership fees will usually include membership of the governing body and insurance against personal injury. If, for some reason, you join a club that is not a member of the governing body, then you'd be well advised to take out your own personal insurance.

The terms used within a Karate club and the customs shown and followed, are all Japanese, and therefore it can take time to become accustomed to what's going on. Don't worry – all you have to do is show politeness and respect and the established *karate-ka* will provide all the help you need.

You can help yourself, too, by having an understanding of general Karate etiquette. Your instructor will tell you about his club in particular, although many of the rules and practises are universal. To begin with, try to familiarize yourself with club etiquette and some of the Japanese terms used.

2

3

2

Toe and ankle exercises ABOVE

1 Flex feet onto outer edges with big toes raised and smaller toes curled under.

2 Roll feet onto inner edges with small toes raised and big toes pushed downward.

3 Raise body weight onto balls of feet and lower slowly to stretch and strengthen the toe and ankle joints.

Knee exercises LEFT

1 Feet no wider apart than shoulder width with both hands on knees.

2 Lower down to squat position, maintaining straight back and arms and rise to starting position. Knees may be rotated in circular fashion while moving through these positions.

1

2

Hips and lower back exercises

Forward and back stretch

1 Spread legs two-and-a-half shoulder widths wide, bend forward with straight back and place elbows as near to floor as is comfortable.

2 Raise upper body, with arms above head and hips thrust forward, before returning to first position

Side stretch

1 Place upper arm behind h lower arm behind back and s sideways, maintaining straigl

2 Transpose position of arm repeat exercise to other side.

1

2

1

2

3

Split exercises

Box split

1 Adopt side split, ensuring that rear foot is turned over in order to avoid excessive knee strain on rear leg.

2 Rotate from side into box split.

3 Rotate into side split in opposite direction.

Seated leg stretch

1 Adopt box split and lower body into seated position.

2 Stretch forwards so underside of chin touches floor.

3 Rotate to right, grasping ankles with both hands and attempt to lower chin past the knee.

4 Rotate and repeat to opposite side.

Three-in-one stretch exercise

1   Spread legs, lowering weight onto left leg and ensuring that right foot is flexed so that the big toe is raised with smaller toes pulled back towards the supporting leg so that the heel protrudes. This position helps to perfect the position of the foot as it should be during impact when used to deliver a side kick.

2   Without raising torso height, twist the hips into the supporting leg while raising the rear leg onto the ball of the foot.

3   Return to face front on heel of right foot, with toes raised. Lean toward supporting foot. Repeat the follow-through exercise to opposite side.

Butterfly stretch LEFT

Sit with feet close together, clasp hands around feet, lower knees to floor and hold position for ten to twenty seconds.

Hamstring stretch BELOW

1 Stand with feet shoulder width apart and stretch upwards with arms above head.

2 Bend forward from the waist, keep legs straight and attempt touching palms of hands to the floor.

1

2

Cat curl

1 For this shoulder strengthening exercise, spread legs and place hands flat on floor.

2 Move downward and forward, maintaining a straight back.

3 Continue the movement through to a straight arm position, stretch upward with chin and look toward ceiling. Return to the beginning position and repeat.

1

2

5

6

3

4

7

Wrist and finger exercises

Gassho LEFT TO RIGHT, ABOVE

1   Stand with feet shoulder width apart, palms of hands together over head.

2   Press palms together, lowering hands in front of chest.

3   Extend hands to front, pointing forward.

4   Draw back into chest.

5   FAR LEFT Lower hands, fingers pointing to floor.

6   LEFT Still pointing downward, pull hands upward toward chest. Throughout whole sequence of movements, ensure that palms remain close together.

Grip exercise RIGHT

Press tips of fingers and thumbs together and sustain pressure for ten to twenty seconds. Repeat several times.

1

2

3

4

5

1

2

Neck exercises LEFT

1   Standing with feet shoulder width apart, hands on hips and with jaw relaxed, lower head backward.

2   Lower head forward.

3   Raise head to face front.

4   Withdraw right shoulder and turn head to left.

5   Repeat to right side.

RIGHT Roll neck in a clockwise direction, then repeat anti-clockwise.

3

1

2

Assisted stretching

1   ABOVE Place heel of foot on partner's shoulder.

2   TOP RIGHT Bend forward and sideways to attempt touching shin of supporting leg with chin. Repeat with other leg.

ABOVE RIGHT Two partners provide support and aid the side stretch of the leg.

RIGHT For this seated leg stretch, sit down with legs as far apart as possible while your partner places his feet just below your knees. Reach forward to clasp hands while partner gently pushes with legs.

Etiquette and Discipline

Whether the place in which you practise Karate is part of a professionally-run club or a modest church hall, it is referred to as a *dojo*. This is a Japanese word of Sanskrit origin and means 'place of practice or enlightenment'.

All *karate-ka* acquire and show the highest respect for the *dojo*. Juniors, seniors and Masters alike remove footwear neatly by the doorway and enter the *dojo* barefooted. At the doorway, every *karate-ka* pauses to *rei* (bow) towards the *dojo kamiza* (focal centre) and exclaims in a clear and positive voice: '*Osu!*' (pronounced 'O-ss'). The word is taken from the phrase *osu-shinobu*, which was an original Samurai greeting. It is an expression of understanding and patience and of the intention to keep going and to endure that which is to come.

The phrase also signifies that a person has emptied their mind of any feelings other than the task in hand. '*Osu!*' is a sound you will hear being made frequently in the *dojo* whenever salutations are exchanged between *karate-ka*. Also, whenever a *karate-ka* enters or leaves the *dojo* for any reason, he pauses at the doorway to bow and exclaim '*Osu!*'

Reishiki

(Etiquette)

Once in the *dojo*, low-grade students are expected to warm up and generally practise their techniques. Any senior grade students present will offer to help any junior seen practising incorrectly. Then a senior will call the class to order prior to the entry of the instructor, and the whole class will line up in grade order.

When lining up in grade order in classical schools, the junior student is always on the right side of the senior student. This was originally so that the *katana* (sword), worked from the left side of the senior, could not be removed. At the same time, the senior could control the drawing of a sword or dagger by the junior on his left.

Any student late for class is still expected to bow at the doorway and call '*Osu!*' before kneeling down at the side of the doorway and waiting for the instructor to accept him or her into the class. Remember, Karate is a dangerous art. If students, or anyone else, were permitted to saunter into the *dojo* unannounced, they could easily be distracting and break the concentration of students engaged in, say, something such as one-step work. That way, accidents can occur. The instructor will also want to ensure that the late student catches up on warming-up exercise routines properly, rather than risking injury by going straight into the performance of techniques.

The instructor is always addressed by students as *sensei*. This word does not translate directly as 'instructor' or 'teacher'. It actually means 'he who has gone before'. So, whatever your instructor demands of you, he has already done before and understands the implications of the action he is asking you to copy. My own teacher always claimed that academics were extremely difficult to teach. This is because Martial Arts have very simple, basic concepts and are generally learned by seeing, copying and experiencing. There is very little need for debating and verbalizing. Full attention and respect must be paid to *sensei* at all times. His commands must be obeyed instantly. At the same time, he will reciprocate with help, advice and patience.

No food should be consumed closer than two hours prior to a Karate session, and eating, drinking and smoking are prohibited in the *dojo*.

Safety and respect

Karate gi's must be kept neat and clean and finger and toe-nails must be trimmed short. Otherwise, a jagged piece of nail can be the cause of serious injury. Skin wounds or even worse, damage to a partner's eye, may be caused, especially during sparring.

For similar reasons of safety, the wearing of all types of jewellery – rings, necklaces, bracelets, hairclips and headbands other than soft elasticated types, and all types of earings or studs – is not allowed. All such sharp adornments need to be removed before entering the *dojo*. If a piece of jewellery, such as a ring or earring cannot be removed, it should be covered with sticking plaster. Every *karate-ka*, junior and senior, contributes to the neatness and hygiene of the *dojo*. Tidying up, putting away equipment, sweeping the floor and keeping the place dust-free, all become automatic habits performed by each and everyone. This generates the awareness that this is your *dojo*, that it belongs to the members, that it is your place of learning and must be respected and cared for. My own club, Bu'sen, typifies this attitude. It is used by some 1,500 people each week and suffers little beyond normal wear and tear. Grafitti and vandalism just don't happen on the premises.

Enforcement of standards of etiquette and discipline is important, but a club also needs to create a relaxed atmosphere that will encourage people to behave in a decent and correct manner. Some procedures may seem strange, but the best thing for the beginner is to take part in the spirit of things, to go along with what's happening within the club environment, and reserve attempts at a greater understanding until later.

Karate *dojo* etiquette has no relationship with rank, either inside or outside the *dojo*. All *karate-ka* are neutralized and made equal as human beings by the wearing of a plain white cotton suit. There is nothing to distinguish one *karate-ka* from another, except the belt which is a recognition of experience. Simple politeness and respect is what it's all about.

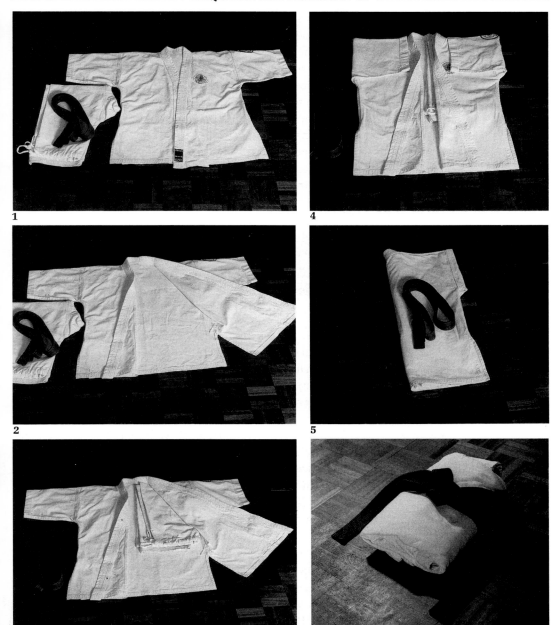

1

2

3

4

5

6

Folding the *Gi*

1 Lay out Karate-gi jacket, folded trousers and belt

2 Fold back one lapel of jacket and open other wide.

3 Place folded trousers in open side of jacket along with any other small pieces of equipment.

4 Close jacket, folding edges in mitre-fashion to match.

5 Fold over jacket in half, lengthways.

6 Tie with belt, leaving ends long if required to provide shoulder strap for carrying.

1

2

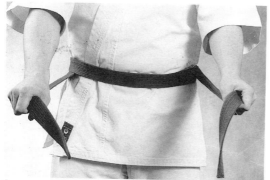

3

4

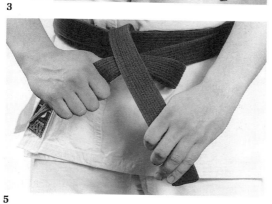

5

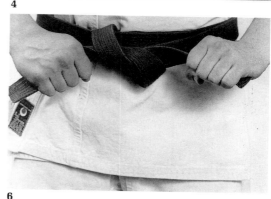

6

7

Tying the belt

TOP LEFT, LEFT TO RIGHT Take centre of *obi* (belt) and wrap around body from front along a line midway between top of pelvic bones and navel.

Pass around back, cross over and return hands to front.

Draw belt tightly toward front.

Take the top section of the belt and pass it under the opposite end which runs beneath, nearest to the body.

Take the top end and pass it over the bottom end.

Draw it upwards and through, pulling both ends tightly in outward directions.

This will form a reef knot, or box knot.

Meditation and Breathing

One thing all students should understand from the outset, is the importance of breathing and the body's inhalation and exhalation of breath. Many Karate schools teach breathing and meditation techniques that are linked directly to *zazen* (controlled breathing exercise in a seated position) and *kinhin* (controlled breathing whilst the body is moving).

Most people do not breathe properly. We generally take too many breaths, inhaling to only a shallow degree so that the air in the lower part of the lung is never fully expelled. However, when a time of stress presents itself, our breathing process automatically speeds up as we prepare ourselves for the 'fight or flight' reaction. Here the body automatically works at peak efficiency but a choice remains: do we remain steadfast and subject ourselves to facing up to whatever opposition confronts us, or do we put our energy into escape? Such decisions have to be made not only during Karate but in many situations in everyday life.

Whatever the circumstances, the body's chemical reactions are the same when subjected to any stress situation. The challenge is to try to control the stressful effects so that we may respond in a strong and positive manner. To do this, the mind must be calm and disciplined and able to centre clearly on the situation, to assess it and decide upon what seems the right course of action, taken in the right sort of manner.

Meisou

(Breathing/ Meditation)

Reactions to stress

Consider how two *karate-ka* may react in different ways to the same situation. I might ask one of my senior Black Belts to demonstrate how to break a brick during a championship tournament. He is of course familiar with the technique and has over a period of time worked through what might be termed 'stressful situations' such as this, calling as it does for him to demonstrate his *tameshiwari* skills before a large audience. Nevertheless, he will prepare his breathing, enter the area, bow to his seniors, prepare the bricks across suitable blocks, calmly consider his technique, concentrate his breath power and then let out his *kiai* (spirit shout) simultaneously as he strikes the brick and the brick breaks.

Now consider how a newly-promoted Black Belt, without the same degree of experience or ability to centre his mind and thoughts on a certain area, might react. As he enters, his first thoughts might be about just how many people are watching him: already his reason for being

Sensei Perry leading a senior Black Belt class in the practice of *seiza*

Sensei Perry seated in *seiza*, practising *zazen*.

Seiza

there and his brick-breaking technique come under pressure. He may then set the bricks up, but wonder whether they are correctly aligned, or balanced – more pressure and distraction from the job in hand.

Next, he worries about the whole lot falling over. Will they break when he strikes them? Will the crowd laugh if he doesn't break them? Throughout this period of escalating stress, his breathing will have become more and more uncontrolled and his feelings of weakness and anxiety multiplied. He would have completely lost the moment for action and be incapable of breaking the brick.

Comparing these two examples, one obvious difference would be the sheer technical superiority of the more experienced Black Belt. More important, though, would have been his trained ability to centre his mind and thoughts upon the task immediately before him. He did not allow into his mind any negative thoughts that would impair the demonstration of his Karate technique. He controlled his breathing. He shut out stress. He executed his technique with perfection.

Similarly, a person placed under the stress of an impending attack must be able to remain relaxed and controlled, able to centre the mind solely on the correct movement to counter the situation in an expert and controlled manner. To begin to develop this ability is to begin the first exercise in *seiza*.

The seiza

The first position the beginner will be required to practise on taking up karate is the *seiza*. This is a kneeling posture with the feet tucked under, and the *karate-ka* must be able to retain it comfortably for any length of time. The *seiza* is the ideal position in which to learn correct breathing and meditation.

Some period of time both at the beginning and end of classes is spent in *seiza*. To adopt *seiza*, the student kneels down with feet tucked under the buttocks. The big toes meet alongside each other and are not tucked one over the other. It is important to keep the back absolutely straight and the shoulders must not droop. Imagine that the body to be suspended by a taught rope, pulling upwards and making the spine stretch and seem longer.

In *seiza* there should be no degree of tension in any part of the body except the *hara* (lower stomach). The position of the hands while in *seiza* can vary from school to school. My own preference is for them to be fisted, with the two sets of knuckles resting one on each thigh and positioned parallel to the front of the chest. Persevere, and with practise the position will become steadily more comfortable to hold for longer periods.

Assume the sitting posture of *seiza* in some quite area where you will not be affected by any noise such as radios, telephones or any other turmoil of modern life. A good time of day is around dawn. Sit in *seiza* and half-close your eyes. Fix your gaze upon a spot on the floor about three feet away. Look at the spot, but don't let it become the focal point of what is a 'stare'. The aim is not to look outwardly *at* the spot, but to almost reflect your sight *off* it, so that you are looking back inwards, into your very self. At the same time, breathe steadily in through your nose and out through your mouth, in a slow and controlled manner. Try not to place any tension on any part of your body. Count 'one' whilst breathing in and 'two' when breathing out. Repeat the breathing pattern, maintaining a mind clear of intrusive thoughts. The moment any idle thought enters your mind, re-commence the breathing count.

In an age when most things which seem to be good are also the most complicated, it's difficult for beginners to accept that so much can be gained from this simple breathing exercise. They naturally believe that their time would be better spent in practise and getting physically strong. In fact, a student should practise *seiza* every day. Beginning with perhaps a ten-minute period, the time may be extended gradually as the student learns to control breathing and to keep the mind clear of intrusive thought.

When a student is able to achieve a period of about twenty minutes without external thoughts coming into the mind, the counting may be disregarded and concentration focused on the development of a slower, deeper breathing pattern. This should include attempts to make the breathing out take twice as long as breathing in.

In my own experience as a competitor, and latterly as an examiner, I

1

2

Nogare (short and long wave breathing)

This breathing exercise can be practised in basic form in order that the Karate exponent may settle his breathing pattern during or after severe exertion.

1 LEFT Breathe in through the nose, filling the lungs by first allowing the belly to rise and then the chest. At the same time, raise the hands palm upwards and pull the elbows back. Hold the breath, ensuring that the abdominal wall is tight.

2 Exhale quickly through the mouth, allowing the stomach to extend. At the same time, turn the palms downward and push toward the floor.

have found those students who take time to learn how to centre their concentration and control breathing patterns are the ones who invariably do better when placed under pressure. Conversely, students who do not understand, or have had no experience of these training methods, tend to avoid situations in which they may feel pressurized, or involved in circumstances over which they have no control. This attitude, of course, is not in the true spirit of *karate-do*.

Contemporary life is such that everyone would benefit from *seiza*, whether *karate-ka* or layman. We are enveloped in a cacophony of engines, telephones, radios, clocks, televisions and bleepers of one sort or another from morning until night. Some time spent quietly each day in order to strengthen one's inner self can only do good to both mind and body and improve one's attitude to life.

The spirit shout

I referred to the experienced Black Belt emitting a loud *kiai* as he struck the brick. It's not possible to translate the word directly into English, but 'spirit shout' or 'breath power' is the generally accepted meaning. Often, the term *kiai* will be applied to a shout that is made by *karate-ka* during fundamental training, perhaps after each punch, or technique. It is emitted as the student expels the last of the air from his lungs in order to help maximize a technique's power of delivery.

The emission of *kiai* encourages a firming up of the *hara* (lower stomach area) and control of the diaphragm upon the completion of a technique. A *karate-ka*'s development of the vocal quality of their own individual *kiai* is important and must not be ignored. I recommend all beginners to get out by the seashore or to some other isolated spot where they can practise until they get the sound right rather than experiment in the *dojo*. Apart from the help it brings to breathing during the delivery of a technique, the dispiriting or crushing affect which something like a double-pitched *kiai* can have upon an opponent should never be under-estimated.

The *kiai* when used in *kata* is usually made at the commencement of a series of techniques. Sometimes it is put into a particular part of the *kata* to emphasize one of its important training aspects. Originally, there was no set *kiai* within *kata* and it was left to come naturally as and when allowed to by the *karate-ka*'s own energy levels.

All that has been described is the understanding and application of *kiai* as a sound. In fact, the full meaning of *kiai* is a more complicated concept. It is the condition of an individual who is for ever in a state of continued readiness and prepared to react instantly to any sudden threat. When such a state of awareness is released there is an explosion of energy from within the person, coinciding with, and helped by, emit-ting the sound of *kiai* – the spirit shout.

I have repeatedly emphasized the importance of developing in parallel both mental and physical qualities, the *ying* and the *yang*. The *kiai* represents the two coming together to create something quite special and complete – *karate-do*. Summing up, I believe that too little emphasis is placed upon the practise and perfection of breathing, of the correct use of *kiai*, or of *kiai* as applied during *kata* or *kumite*. This may be due to the misunderstandings which prevail about *kiai* and what it's really all about. Once a rational understanding of *kiai* has been grasped, it becomes possible to *kiai* in either a fast or slow manner – or, finally, even in a *silent* manner!

Postures and Stances

Kamae
(Posture)

Stances may be considered the base from which all offensive and defensive techniques are launched. They are not, however, anywhere near as static as the name might infer. They are constantly being changed in the course of *kata* or *kumite*, providing the means of moving from one position to another during combat. Much time should be spent on holding stances and learning how to move from one to another. As the student starts to learn *kata*, the necessary changes from one stance to another will become apparent. They will be practised repeatedly until they blend into sequences of fluid movements gone through with whatever changes and variations are necessary.

Because of variable body types and build, certain stances will be found to suit certain individuals better than others. Again, the student must be patient and persevere. Until trained in *all* the stances, he or she will be ill-equipped to pick and choose. At the same time, beginners must be aware that, providing the basic physiology of the movement into a stance is adhered to, they should not be so concerned with positioning that they fail to produce a flowing and relaxed movement.

Another difficult concept for the beginner student to understand, is that the strongest of all stances in karate is, in fact, no stance at all! Again, this is something which will only become understood with Karate experience. It should not deter anyone from diligently working towards firming up on basic stances and allowing their body to strengthen accordingly for more advanced *kata* and general training.

The stances shown encompass the basics of stability and strength required in Karate from beginner to advanced level.

1 *Shizen tai (natural stance)*
Normal standing posture with knees naturally bent.

2 *Heisoku dachi (closed stance)*
Weight distributed 50–50 between both feet with feet parallel, heels and toes together.

1

2

3

4

5

6

7

8

3 *Musubi dachi (open stance)*
Weight distributed 50–50 between both feet while heels are together with toes pointing out at forty-five degrees.

4 *Fudo dachi (formal stance)*
Feet shoulder width apart with equal weight distribution. Hands held fisted with forearms parallel to the floor.

5 *Yoi dachi (prepared stance)*
Feet on a parellel line, legs and stomach held under tension, hands fisted and pulling down towards floor.

6 *Zenkutsu dachi (forward leaning stance)*
Length of stance about two shoulder widths while width of stance is maintained at one shoulder width. Front knee directly over the ankle, while back leg is held straight with rear foot pointing out at forty-five degrees. Weight distributed 60–70% on front leg, remainder on back leg.

7 *Sanchin dachi (diamond stance)*
Feet shoulder width apart with toes of rear foot and heel of front foot in line. Feet turned inward, knees bent over feet and weight distributed 60% on front and 40% on rear leg. Note that on reaching intermediate level in Karate, it is more favourable to straighten the back foot but still maintaining the inward turn on the right foot.

8 *Kokutsu dachi (back leaning stance)*
Weight distributed 70% on back leg, 30% on front, with knees bending over feet. The stance is approximately one shoulder-width long with the feet approximately four inches apart as seen from the front.

9 *Nekoashi dachi (cat stance)*
Ninety per cent of the weight is taken on the back foot while the front foot is placed approximately twelve inches forward and raised as high as possible on the ball of the foot. Both knees are bent over the feet with hips pushed back.

10 *Shiko dachi (sumo stance)*
Feet approximately two shoulder widths apart with toes pointing outwards at 45°. Knees are pushed outward over the feet in order to obtain a perpendicular line to the floor with the shins. Weight distributed 50–50 on both feet.

11 *Kiba dachi (straddle stance)*
Parallel feet placed approximately two shoulder widths apart with toes pointing forward. Knees pushed outwards over feet. Back straight as possible.

12 *Moroachi dachi (one-step stance)*
One foot placed in front of other so that heel of front foot and toes of back foot are in line. Toes point straight forward.

13 *Kake dachi (hook stance)*
Rear foot is placed one foot past support foot and acts as a brake when making quick transitions from this stance. Both knees bent. To check position of feet, rotate 180° towards the rear foot and both feet will then be positioned as for *moroachi dachi*. Weight distribution 60% on front leg, 40% on rear.

14 *Tsuriashi dachi (crane stance)*
Weight is 100% on supporting leg. Other foot is raised with big toe up and smaller toes pushed down so that the outer edge of the foot is parallel to the floor. Rib cage is raised, hips are lowered.

9

10

11

12

13

14

Our Natural Weapons

The basic weapons of which we make use in modern Karate are those provided to us by nature – our hands, feet, arms, legs, knees, elbows, and wrists. Most instructors begin by showing students how to make a fist. This provides a basic introduction to a full understanding of hand techniques in general. I encourage my beginner students to regard the arm as the extension tube of a cylinder vacuum cleaner. Different attachments to cope with different jobs performed by the vacuum cleaner are fixed to the end of the tube, and these can be seen as the different types of hand, or fist, that can be made to strike most effectively at different parts of an opponent's body. Just as the vacuum cleaner's tools can be changed on the end of the tube to enable the user to penetrate small areas or cover large ones, so is the shape of the hand, or fist, changed to deliver differing techniques to various areas of an opponent's body.

Nature provides most of the weak areas of the body with a degree of protective muscle or protects them by making us react very quickly to keep them out of harm's way. So, opponents will automatically flinch and move their heads away if they are looking at you as you attack, say, a vulnerable eye. The only way you're going to be able to strike at the eye is to attack the instant your opponent's attention is distracted by, say, your blocking of one of his attacks. In that split second, the eye will be vulnerable and exposed to your attacking strike.

Buki
(Natural Weapons)

Probably the most famous weapon in the Karate arsenal is the knife-hand, or Karate chop. This is used so extensively throughout the media as an apparently magical method of felling any opponent to the ground under almost any circumstances, but the technique shown on the screen has little to do with real Karate. Perhaps it is a good thing to keep the 'chop' at this superficial level so far as the total community is concerned, otherwise tutored but undisciplined practitioners would be using it with deadly effect to settle everyday differences of opinion. The only way to be really effective in your ability to fell an opponent with a single blow, is to perfect a full repertoire of hand strikes, blocks, elbow strikes, and kicks.

No one technique is effective, or can be applied, under all circumstances, as inferred by the media's over-exposure of that familiar Karate chop. Each technique, including the chop, is designed to fit a particular set of circumstances whether encountered in a contest or street-corner attack. For instance, when fighting a taller opponent at close range, a head-butt is effective because the strong part of your head is attacking towards his weaker jaw, or the bridge of his nose. Reverse the situation and you can imagine how the head-butt is not an effective technique for use by the taller man who can only butt downwards towards the strong part of your head.

How our other limbs and body extremities are used as natural weapons is demonstrated throughout this book either by me or by some of my students. It is worth emphasizing that kicking techniques require the exponent to have strong ankle joints and good control of the toes to be really effective. The strength and mobility of ankles, and toes in particular, can so easily be overlooked. When most beginners first exercise toes in the *dojo*, moving them into set positions, they have little or no control over them. I have met Karate Masters with toes so mobile that they have been able to use them to grasp hold of an opponent with much the same strength as fingers.

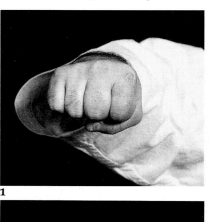
1

2

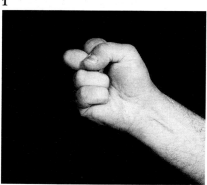
3

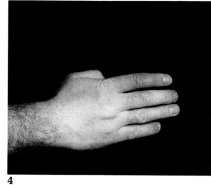
4

Hands

1   *Seiken (fist)*
The first two knuckles are used in striking with a Karate fist.

2   *Uraken (back fist)*
The strike is delivered with the back part of the first two knuckles.

3   *Ipponken (middle knuckle fist)*
The middle finger is pushed forward with the thumb placed against it.

4   *Shuto (knife hand)*
The striking area is from above the wrist to the middle of the edge of the palm. The hand is spread, fingers held under tension, the thumb tucked in.

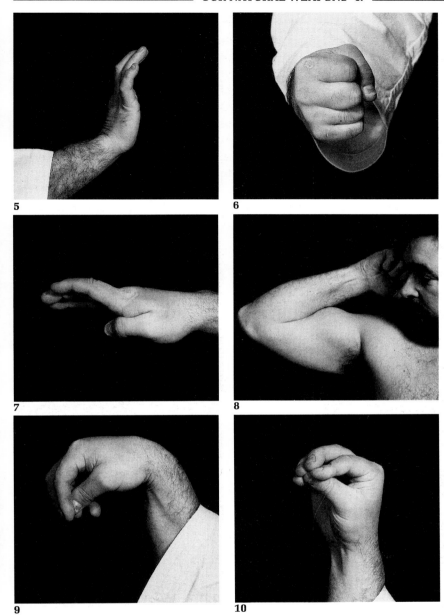

5 *Shotei (palm heel)*
The striking area is the lower part of the palm. The hand is kept flexed back and the thumb tucked in.

6 *Tettsui (hammer fist)*
The fist is clenched tight. Striking surface is the area between the little knuckle and the wrist.

7 *Haito (inner knife hand)*
The striking surface is from the first knuckle of the index finger, along the edge of the hand to the wrist.

8 *Hijiate (elbow strike)*
This is delivered with the point of the elbow.

9 *Koken (wrist)*
The wrist is pulled down with the thumb touching the middle and ring fingers. The striking surface is the top of the wrist.

10 *Keiko (chicken beak)*
Finger tips are gathered around the thumb to form a strike surface which will fit into an opponent's eye socket.

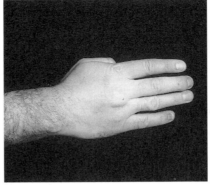

11

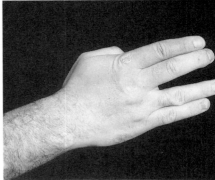

12

13

14

11 *Nukite (spear hand)*
Fingers held straight and under
tension, with thumb tucked in. Tips of
fingers provide striking surface.

12 *Nihon nukite (split spear hand)*
As with *nukite* but with fingers
centrally divided to provide striking
surface against opponent's eyes.

13 *Toho (sword hand)*
Striking areas are tips of the index
finger and thumb. Upon striking an
opponent's throat, *toho* is then used to
make a grab.

14 *Toho* applied to opponent's
throat.

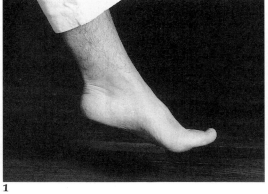

1

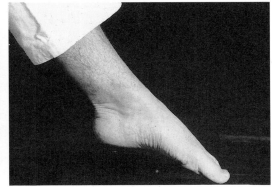

2

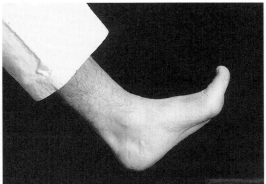

3

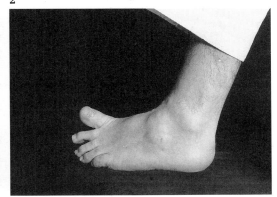

4

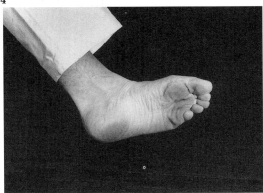

5

Feet

1   *Chusoku (ball of foot)*
Striking surface is the area just below
the underside of the toes when the
toes are pulled back.

2   *Haisoku (instep)*
Extend food forward, pointing toes
down. The striking surface is the
instep, or top of the foot.

3   *Kakato (heel)*
Pull the foot back to push the heel
forward and provide a striking
surface which is beneath the heel.

4   *Sokuto (knife foot)*
Pull up the big toe, curl smaller toes
down and flex the ankle downwards.
Striking with outside of foot

5   *Teisoku (sole of foot)*
Flex the ankle inward and curl in toes
to present the sole of the foot as a
striking surface.

Head

Atama (head)

TOP The striking surface is usually the centre point of the front hair line, although the back or side of the crown may be used against the softer part of an opponent's face. Shown there is the back of the head being used against an opponent who has grabbed from behind.

Knee

Hiza (knee)

The raised knee is bent, with toes and foot of the striking leg pointing downwards. Strike surface is the top of the knee, here being used against an opponent's head.

Making a fist

There are many ways of making a fist and quite a range of different sorts of weapons, each fitted for particular types of attacks, can be formed with the hand. Whatever the form, though, remember to perfect techniques with both right and left hands so that either is capable of landing an effective blow.

I recommend beginning with a study of *seiken* (striking with the first two knuckles of a forefist). In this particular formation, all four fingers are folded firmly inwards with the thumb gripped tightly over the first two fingers. The back of the hands runs on a parallel line to the forearm, so that the first two knuckles protrude forwards. There is a slight outward turn of the hand so that the first knuckle is almost in line with the edge of the forearm.

Kobushi
(Making a Fist)

Having formed the fist properly, it must now be delivered as a blow. For as long as anyone remembers, it has been taught that the effectiveness of a Karate punch depends upon the inward spiralling of the arm during delivery. This is accompanied by a simultaneous snapping withdrawal, moving in the opposite direction towards your own body, of the free hand not delivering the punch. Scientific testing has shown that the twisting, spiralling movement on its own, actually slows down the delivery. However, the ultimate completion of the spiral, combined with the simultaneous pull-back reverse action of the free hand, maximizes the forward thrust of the blow.

Having learned how to make a fist and become familiar with the principles of delivery, the *karate-ka* must next learn to relax the arm and fist and only to tighten up immediately prior to impact. Failure to do this will slow down the technique. Additionally, any premature tensing up of the arm will provide an opponent with an early warning of attack.

The hands need to be conditioned over a period of time in order to perform *seiken*. Training methods begin with press-ups from clenched fists supporting your weight on a hard floor. Then, progress to walking on the knuckles, legs supported wheelbarrow fashion as your partner holds your feet off the floor. After some six to nine months of regular work on the knuckles in this manner, a student may move on to using the *makiwari* (punching post).

Using the makiwari

Regular punching work on the *makiwari* gradually creates a callus between the first two knuckle joints on the front corner of the fist, as the tendons which normally run over them are pushed to new positions on either side of the joints. As the callus develops, it begins to provide a certain amount of protective padding over the first two joints. At this point, care must be taken that these protective layers do not become so large that they 'screw out' and cause the hand more damage than they afford protection.

Throughout all the work you do on conditioning the fists, whether press-ups or on the *makiwari*, apply most pressure to the first knuckle. Otherwise, the middle knuckle will always tend to absorb most impact and consequently become over-enlarged. This will result in an imbalance to your fist and therefore a weakness.

After going through a fairly long and arduous process of conditioning, cartilage will build up inside the hand, fusing the first two knuckles into one solid joint. Finally, the day will come when the instructor will allow you to attempt punching your way into concrete, wood or other hard substances, without sustaining injury to your hand or knuckle joints. Only when you've achieved this by yourself, will you become aware of the reality of the power behind a properly prepared Karate punch.

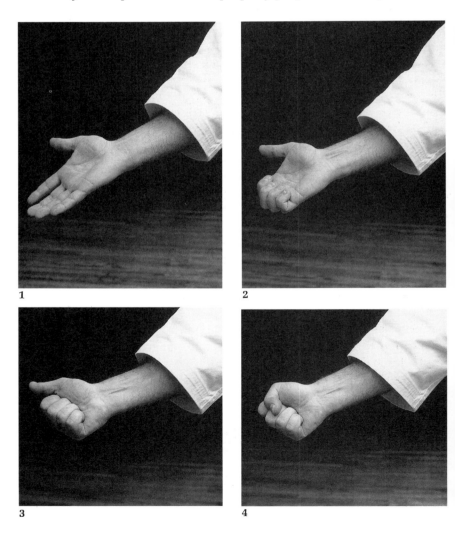

1

2

3

4

1

2

3

4

Making a fist

1 from the open hand.

2 Curl the fingers in tightly.

3 Tighten them into the palm.

4 Wrap over the thumb.

Delivering a punch

1 Adopt *sanchin dachi* stance. Place right fist out with palm down, at sternum height; at same time withdraw left fist, with palm uppermost.

2 Begin withdrawing right fist in spiral movement while starting to deliver a punch with the left fist, also moving in a spiral.

3 This is the important cross-over stage of movement showing both fists in identical positions.

4 The right fist is now totally withdrawn and the left fist has been extended in a spiralling movement to complete the punch. Note the slight outward turn of the extended fist, ensuring that *seiken* is the striking surface.

1

2

Knuckle conditioning

Two-fisted press-ups, one fisted and finger tip press-ups are all hand conditioning exercises. Finger tip exercises are important because the small bones and tendons in the back of the hand need to be strong enough to absorb intensive shock.

3

Attacking and Defensive Techniques

Having prepared properly and become familiar with the basics of Karate, the student will be ready to move on to learning fundamental attacking and defensive techniques using arms, legs, hands and feet. It's an important time for the beginner, but one which can easily become complex and even daunting if not kept in a proper perspective.

The beginner student will be told by an instructor to do this and do that, to do it this way or that way. There will be much repetition and sometimes the student will be asked to perform what seems to be impossible tasks. During this period, students can do no more than follow instructors to the best of their individual abilities. Strenuous, tedious, perhaps even boring on occasions, it must be remembered that the instructor went through the same procedures and as *sensei* is asking you to perform nothing which he has not undergone during his Karate career. Remember the meaning of the word *sensei*. The instructor has been here before and, as he will lead the student to realize, a grasp of the fundamentals is the reward for concentration, repetition and dedication.

A thrust, or any technique, eventually becomes a natural movement requiring no conscious thought to put it into instant action. An easy comparison is with the baby who begins first to stand upon its feet, then to totter and thereafter to walk in a well-balanced manner.

仕掛け技　手、腕

Te Ude Shikake Waza

(Attacking Hand & Arm Techniques)

During a Karate class, a basic punch will be repeated time and time again until students become utterly exhausted by its repeated practice. The technique then becomes ingrained both mentally and physically.

There should be no feeling by students that they are enduring pain and following blindly. Such an attitude would enable them to make excuses and not train in a persevering and proper manner. Instead, they need encouragement to realize that all efforts are cumulative and objective. If they become able to resist thinking about personal anguish suffered during practice and get on with their training despite this, then they will have taken the first step towards the casting off of personal ego.

*Jodan tsuki
(upper thrust)*

ABOVE The delivery of *jodan tsuki* to an opponent's face.

TOP LEFT *Chudan tsuki (middle thrust)*

TOP RIGHT *Gyaku tsuki (reverse punch)*
Like the forward thrust, but more powerful because the body
twists as the punch is delivered with the fist opposite the leading
leg.

RIGHT *Uraken jodan uchi (upper back fist strike)*

LEFT *Uraken yoko uchi (side back fist strike)*

ABOVE The delivery of a *uraken jodan uchi* or a *uraken yoko uchi* to the bridge of an opponent's nose.

FAR LEFT Starting position for *uraken hizo uchi (spleen strike)*

LEFT Completed *uraken hizo uchi* after which striking hand returns to position beneath other hand.

ABOVE *Uraken hizo uchi* being delivered to opponent's spleen.

LEFT *Morote tsuki (double thrust)*

ABOVE Application of *morote tsuki* showing how the upper arm thrust may be used also to deflect an opponent's attack to your own face.

FAR LEFT Staring position for *ago tsuki* (*jaw thrust*)

LEFT Twist upper part of body to maximize power of delivery.

ABOVE Application of *ago tsuki* to opponent's jaw.

LEFT *Shita tsuki (inverted punch)* showing centre line of delivery.

ABOVE Application of *shita tsuki* to opponent's solar plexus.

LEFT *Shotei uchi (palm heel strike)*

ABOVE Application of *shotei uchi* to opponent's chin.

FAR LEFT Hands withdrawn in preparation for *shuto yoko ganmen uchi (knife hand strike to head)*

LEFT Technique completed in axe-swinging motion.

ABOVE Application of *shuto yoko ganmen uchi* to side of opponent's neck or head.

LEFT *Shuto sokotsu uchi (knife hand strike to collar bone)*

ABOVE Application of *shuto sokotsu uchi* to opponent's collar bone.

LEFT *Shuto yoko uchi (side knife hand strike)*

ABOVE Application of *shuto yoko uchi* to opponent's throat.

LEFT *Hijiate jodan (upper elbow strike)*

ABOVE Application of *hijiate jodan* to opponent's jaw or head is made in a circular action.

LEFT *Hijiate age* (*rising elbow strike*) showing outward turn of wrist of striking arm to ensure safety of one's own face.

ABOVE Application of *hijate age* to opponent's chin.

LEFT *Haito jodan uchi* (*ridge hand upper strike*)

ABOVE Application of *jodan uchi* to opponent's mastoid.

LEFT Ippon ken uchi jodan (middle knuckle strike to upper area).

ABOVE Application of *ippon ken uchi jodan* to opponent's trachea.

LEFT Koken uchi (wrist strike)

ABOVE Application of *koken uchi* to opponent's jaw or neck.

LEFT Nukite jodan uchi (spear hand upper strike)

ABOVE Application of nukite jodan uchi to opponent's throat.

LEFT Keiko uchi (chicken beak strike)

ABOVE Application of keiko uchi to opponent's eye.

手、腕
応じ技

Te Ude Ouji Waza
(Defensive Hand &
Arm Techniques)

1

2

3

4

Defensive Hand and Arm Techniques

Jodan uke (upper block)

Jodan uke is one of the first defensive hand and arm techniques taught to students. It affords protection against straight punches, hooks and roundhouse kicks.

1 The first movement in *jodan uke* is to cover the body with the blocking arm, moving across the body.

2 The blocking arm effectively sweeps through the whole upper body area.

3 Completion of the block showing how the withdrawing arm is pulled back extremely fast and hard, to turn the body through 45°.

ABOVE Application of *jodan uke* against a face punch.

1

2

3

4

Gedan barai (downward parry)

1   Raise fist to upper ear, covering lower body with opposite fist.

2   Fist lowers in sweeping action with great emphasis on fast pull-back of other fist.

3   Completed block shows arm just outside of body line, with shoulders angled at 45°.

When applying the downward parry against a kick, always attempt to use this block against the outer side of an opponent's shin. This block may be used also against hand strikes and grabbing techniques.

1

Uchi uke (inside block)

1 In preparation for full basic block, place the blocking hand beneath the extended opposite arm in readiness for strong pull-back.

2 Take blocking arm forward in circular motion as opposite arm is withdrawn.

3 Elbow of blocking arm is stopped in line with outside of body and fist is locked in to form a strong blocking technique. Again, shoulders are pulled back by withdrawing hand to angle of 45°.

ABOVE Opponent's punch is effectively blocked by a left-hand *uchi uke*.

3

1

2

3

Soto uke (outside block)

1 Right hand raised behind head with left fist up by shoulder in preparation to block.

2 Right hand is thrown to front in a semi-circular twisting action.

3 On completion of the block, the fist is fully twisted to add to the power of deflection. The withdrawing hand again pulls the body to an angle of 45°. It is important that the blocking arm elbow and forearm move across to screen the whole of the body.

ABOVE Application of *soto uke* shown here in use against an opponent's *chudan tsuki* attack.

Here is a series of more advanced blocks shown as completed techniques with examples of their use against various attacks.

TOP LEFT *Shotei jodan uke (palm heel upper block)*

TOP RIGHT *Shotei jodan uke* used against face attack.

LEFT *Shotei gedan uke (palm heel lower block)*

ABOVE *Shotei gedan uke* used against a front kick

TOP LEFT _Koken jodan uke (wrist block)_

TOP RIGHT _Koken jodan uke_ used against a front hand punch.

LEFT _Haito uchi uke (ridge hand outside block)_

ABOVE _Haito uchi uke_ used against a reverse punch.

Circular blocks

The most powerful blocks in Karate are made in circular motion with the arms, against straight linear attacks. They can also be used for controlling opponents when they attempt to make certain grabs.

Kaiten uke (circular or rolling block)

1 Right arm is positioned and left hand placed palm down under the elbow.

2 Elbow of right hand driven downward as left hand is raised in preparation to execute circular action.

3, 4 & 5 Both hands work simultaneously to execute full circular movements. Hands must be kept forward of the body, moving as if pushing against an imaginary window.

6 On completion of full circular movement, both hands are pulled back to the body, palms positioned as shown.

7

8

7   Hands now thrust forward.

8   Hands move to execute *shotei jodan* and *gedan uchi* in simultaneous movements.

ABOVE *Kaiten uke* being used against a double punching attack.

ABOVE RIGHT *Kaiten uke* movement culminates in an arm locking technique which may be used to control an opponent or to execute a throw which would break his arm.

1

2

5

6

Shuto mawashi uke (knife hand roundhouse block)

1 Adopt a *kokutsu dachi* stance with right hand forward.

2 Swing both hands down toward right knee.

3 In continuous action, draw both hands back to left hip, right hand behind.

4 Raise both hands upward.

5 Continue to raise hands above head anti-clockwise.

6 Continue moving hands forward and down through circular movement.

7 Withdraw left hand towards solar plexus while making downward cut with right hand.

8 Completed block leaves left hand on solar plexus, palm up, and right hand held out at approximately jaw height. The left hand must not withdraw any further than the line below the left ear as this will misalign the trapezius muscles and result in loss of power in the forward hand block

3

4

7

8

TOP A double-handed parry against a front kick.

ABOVE A *shuto uke* is applied against a punching attack.

1   Application of *shuto mawashi uke* against a wrist attack. Opponent grabs wrist.

2   Defender's arm is swung upward in *shuto mawashi* movement with left hand placed just above opponent's elbow joint.

3   Opponent pulled forward and round into an arm lock which may be used to control him.

1

2

3

足

Ashi Shikake Waza

(Attacking Foot &
Leg Techniques)

仕掛け技

Attacking Leg and Foot Techniques

Before engaging in any practice of kicking techniques, be certain to warm up thoroughly the hips, legs and particularly the ankle joints. This helps avoid tears or strains which may hinder training schedules.

Attacks with the feet are generally considered to be five to seven times more powerful than corresponding hand and arm techniques. Therefore, the emphasis during kicking practice must be placed upon correct position,

accuracy and speed. Providing proper attention is made to these three aspects, the mass of the leg will ensure powerful impact.

All kicks are shown being executed from *fudo dachi* (formal stance) and I recommend practice in this way in order that the legs and hips are worked to their maximums. Afterwards, the kicking techniques may be executed in basic and fighting stances.

Mae keage (front pendulum kick)
Begin by adopting *fudo dachi* (formal stance), ensuring that while fists are held tight, the neck and shoulders are kept relaxed both prior to, and during, the execution of all kicks practised.

Swing right leg up in full forward arc, attempting the place knee of kicking leg to the shoulder. This kick serves little purpose in a combat situation but provides an extremely good exercise in flexibility and balance and thus will benefit all kicking techniques.

1

2

Hiza geri (knee kick)

1   Assume *fudo dachi*.

2   Drive knee of attacking leg upward in forward arc ensuring downward pointing foot position.

RIGHT Application shows knee kick used against head of opponent.

1

2

Kin geri (groin attack)

1   From *fudo dachi* stance, raise knee whilst at same time ensuring that the kicking foot is correctly positioned and the ankle firmed prior to delivery of the kick. This will ensure that the opponent's groin is struck with the instep.

2   Leg is extended with snapping action, the striking foot being returned as quickly as possibly to prevent it being held by an opponent.

Application of *kin geri* shows how the instep is driven into opponent's groin. In close-quarter combat, the same technique may be delivered with the shin.

1

2

Mae geri (front kick)

1 From *fudo dachi* raise knee above waist height, ensuring that the sole of the kicking foot is held parallel to the floor with toes pulled back.

2 The striking foot is thrust forward with toes pulled fully back to expose the striking surface, which is the ball of the foot.

RIGHT Application of *mae geri* shown in an attack to an opponent's stomach, demonstrating the tremendous range advantage of kicks over punches.

1

2

Mae kakato geri (front heel kick)

1   From *fudo dachi* raise the knee of the attacking leg with toes and foot pulled back to project the heel.

2   Drive attacking foot forward with thrusting action, ensuring that foot and toes remain pulled well back.

Application of *mae kakato geri* shows its use against an opponent's double wrist grab.

1

2

Yon-ju-go kakato geri (45° heel kick)

1 From *fudo dachi* raise the knee just above the waist height, drawing the foot and toes back to expose the heel. Angle the shin of the attacking leg.

2 Drive the kicking leg outwards through a semi-circular movement so that the foot will strike obliquely across an opponent's leg.

RIGHT Application shows use of *yon-ju-go kakato geri* against the supporting leg of an opponent whose own attacking foot has been blocked.

1

2

Kanzetsu geri (joint kick)

1 From *fudo dachi* assume *tsuruashi dachi* (crane stance) ensuring that the sole of the kicking foot is parallel to the floor with big toe raised and smaller toes curled under to make *sokuto* (knife foot).

2 Attacking foot driven to side of body with a stamping action.

RIGHT Application shows *kanzetsu geri* being delivered to an opponent's knee joint.

1

2

Yoko geri sokuto (side kick)

1 From *fudo dachi* assume *tsuruashi dachi* with foot drawn back into *sokuto*.

2 Thrust attacking foot with an upward, semi-circular movement, ensuring that the hips twist simultaneously with the culmination of the kick.

RIGHT Application of *yoko geri sokuto* shown in an attack to opponent's throat area. Note how the knife edge of the attacking foot is applied with maximum striking efficiency.

1

2

Mawashi geri (roundhouse kick)

1 From *fudo dachi* raise knee of attacking leg and ensure that the inner thigh is parallel to the floor.

2 Drive the attacking foot around and upward in a semi-circular movement.

RIGHT Application of *mawashi geri* shows it as a counter to a punching attack, demonstrating clearly how the *chusoku* (ball of the foot) provides the striking surface.

1

2

Ushiro mawashi geri (rear roundhouse kick)

1   From *fudo dachi* raise right knee while turning head to look to rear, ensuring that the weight is taken on the ball of the supporting foot.

2   Turn the body as the attacking leg is uncoiled to hook with the foot against an opponent's head area.

RIGHT *Ushiro mawashi geri* being delivered to opponent's jaw.

2

Ushiro geri (back kick)

1   From *fudo dachi* raise the knee, pulling toes and foot back towards the knee to expose the heel.

2   Thrust attacking foot to the rear, leaning upper body over the knee of supporting leg.

RIGHT Application of *ushiro geri* against an opponent's mid-section.

足

応じ技

Ashi Ou Oji Waza
(Defensive Foot &
Leg Techniques)

Defensive Leg and Foot Techniques

All kicks may be used in either attack
or defence, and some time should be
spent learning how to block, jam,
sweep and redirect an opponent's
attacks by using your legs and feet.

This will enable you to defend the
upper half of your body with your
hands and thus make you less
susceptible to attacks which are
switched by an opponent from lower
to upper level.

Here are some examples of the
defensive application of foot and leg
techniques.

A *mae geri* is jammed by a *yoko geri*.

RIGHT A low *mawashi geri* is blocked by a *suni uke* (shin block)

BELOW An *ushiro geri* is pushed away with *mae kakato geri*.

LEFT An *ashi barai* is defended against with *yon-ju-go kakato geri*.

BELOW An opponent's *mawashi geri* is deflected by use of *soto mawashi keage*.

RIGHT An opponent's *mawashi geri* is covered while his supporting leg is attacked with a low *suni-geri*.

BELOW An opponent's *yoko geri* is countered with a *soto mawashi geri*

The Importance of *Kata*

The word *kata* means form, or shape, and it is the collective name we give to any group of Karate exercises which relate together and combine in the creation of a form. *Kata*, therefore, is the performance in sequence of certain stances, each stance representing a recognized movement used to defend oneself in a particular circumstance.

Kata
(Form)

There are many different *kata*, each one comprising separate sets of movements from one stance to another and each suited for self-defence and counter-attack in a variety of situations. It is worth noting, though, that every *kata* begins with a defensive blocking technique and this reinforces the philosophy of *karate ni senti nashi* (no first attack in Karate).

Proven techniques once used in ancient battlefield combat are to be found hidden away in the *kata*. There are even techniques that run in sequence, each one designed to expose a different part of the opponent's body to follow-up if a continued attack proves necessary. It would be fair to say that more than fifty *kata*, designed by the old Masters, are available to modern practitioners of Karate. Many more have been lost over the years, largely due to the secrecy which certain schools maintained concerning their own techniques. There is of course an official list of *kata* that may be used in World Union of Karate Organization *kata* competitions.

A lifetime's study and research has gone into the selection of the eighteen *kata* taught and practised within my own school and I see no reason why changes should be made even today to their basic physiological principles. There is nothing preventing a modern Karate Master from creating his own *kata* if he feels it necessary. However, it has been my experience that any and every type of *kata* technique is already somewhere in existence and is simply waiting for any one who cares to take it up.

Kata are given names by whichever Master creates them. In recounting the history of Karate I have already mentioned two which were named after early Masters, *Wansu* and *Kusanku*. Other names may reflect the type or spirit of the *kata* or sometimes the areas in which they originated.

Approaches *to* kata

A *kata* is usually taught in three stages, taking for granted that the basic techniques applied in the *kata* have first been mastered in *kihon* (working on a single technique before putting it within a group). The number of techniques, or stances, vary from one *kata* to another. The stages are:

1: Break the *kata* down into segments and learn each part separately until, bit by bit, the whole *kata* is built up into a single unit. This would normally take about a month for the average student working on a basic *kata*.

2: The *kata* is then moulded together, any weaknesses corrected and polish is put on the rhythm and timing.

3: The third stage is acquiring a full understanding of the application of the techniques and movements learned.

As the student passes through these various stages of learning, repeated and concentrated control of movement will bring about a realization that each performance can be a unique experience; that a good *kata* rids the exponent of self-consciousness or nervousness and brings about a mental calm. Each *kata* requires years of experience to perfect and the aim is to be able to execute a *kata* without having to remind oneself what to do next.

The ultimate is to complete the *kata* and have no realization of what you have actually done until someone tells you how excellent it all was. That is the moment of the coming together of your mental and physical being in the purest possible way. It underlines my claim that *kata* is the heart of *karate-do*, while the fighting elements which follow are its soul.

It is during such an ideal and fulfilling performance of a *kata* that a student must concentrate and rid the mind of any everyday traumas. Otherwise, problems not related to Karate will show up in the form of movements not properly controlled, bad timing and poor rhythms. A *kata* performance is a reflection of our true selves, its movements are the mirror of our mind and through this we come to experience the meaning of 'moving zen'.

Concerning the more purely physical aspects of *kata* in general, some schools show *kata* as an application in which the person performing the *kata* is battling against more than one imaginary opponent. This is often a popular, though unrealistic, demonstration piece at major tournaments. Anyone with a true depth of knowledge soon comes to realize that any *kata* consists of a group of movements that can be applied in many different ways and in different and even extreme circumstances.

For instance, you are not necessarily going to meet someone your own size in all fighting situations. You will be fighting short and stocky opponents, some small and thin, others tall and heavy and vice versa. Don't be alarmed – there are variations within each *kata* of techniques for dealing with them all. Also, it's not only the opponents who may vary – the surfaces upon which you may be called upon to fight may vary from the smooth wooden floor of a *dojo* to an outdoor situation in which you're on rough, uneven ground. In fact, one *kata*, named *kanku-dai* (signifying the skyward gaze with which the *kata* begins), actually includes a movement which teaches the exponent to pick up dirt from the floor and throw it in an opponent's face before making a second attack.

Kata *and* kumite

It's quite common for Karate practitioners to become labelled as either 'fighters' or 'kata performers', inferring that neither is not much good at the other. In my experience, my best students who have been placed amongst the first three in *kata*, have fared equally well in *kumite* and vice versa.

There is, of course, a noticeable difference between the abilities of someone who does *kata* purely to look good and impress competition judges, and someone who practises *kata* to further their understanding of Karate in order that they may acquire stance practice and develop the application of real power. Any movement in Karate can be made to look impressive to the untrained eye. However, after training in the correct manner and gaining a deeper understanding of *kata*, you will soon realize by watching a person, even as they walk onto the mat and bow before they start their *kata*, what to expect from them.

The idea that *kata* and *kumite* are different is refuted by the fact that movements applied in *kata* all relate to real-life situations. Many techniques included in *kata* are regarded as so dangerous that they are now banned from competition and have begun to be phased out from general club practice.

The kata *today*

With modern-style Karate seeking acceptance in the sporting world, it's worth comparing photographs of Masters of only fifty years ago performing Karate with the various styles that have since transformed certain movements into gymnastics. The idea has been to make Karate appear more visually impressive and possibly more demanding. These changes are not necessarily a good thing, because not everyone wishing to take up Karate is capable of such athleticism. In fact, the older style *kata* included very few kicks, with hardly any above waist height.

When the *kata* were first developed to be applied in a self-defensive manner, individuals were trained to fight against unskilled or unscientific opponents. Nowadays, Karate is moving along the road of *karate-ka* fighting *karate-ka*, and the low kicks of years ago are found to have their limitations when skill meets with skill. Therefore, the techniques have been expanded to suit present-day contest work. This is acceptable, so long as the emphasis remains upon defensive and disabling techniques as opposed to the more flashy, showy competition techniques.

Finally, *kata* is without doubt the heart of all training, with all other aspects of Karate latched onto it. The perfection of *kata* is something which should become every *karate-ka*'s lifelong endeavour. Even now, after years of study, I find that with continual practise my understanding of various techniques increases time and time again.

All kata pictures are in order left to right from top to bottom of each page.

Taikoyoko soni ichi, or 'the *kata* of all directions', forms the basis of training from beginner right through to Dan Grade level. It features one stance (*zenkutsu dachi*), one basic block (*mae gedan barai*) and one punch (*chudan tsuki*).

Assume *fudo dachi* stance

Raise hands to ears . . .

. . . before *yoi-dachi*

Turn left 90° into *zenkutsu dachi*

Block *mae gedan barai*

Step forward and punch *chudan tsuki.*

Move front foot to rear through 180°

Block *mae gedan barai*

Move left foot forward and punch *chudan tsuki*

Turn left

Block *mae gedan barai*

Right foot forward and punch *mae chudan tsuki*

Move left foot forward and punch *chudan tsuki*

Move forward with right foot, punch *chudan tsuki* and emit loud *kiai*

Cover groin with right fist, placing left fist to right ear, back turning on left foot.

Block left *mae gedan barai*

Move right foot forward and punch *chudan tsuki*

Cover groin with left fist, placing right fist to left ear, back turning with right foot.

Block right *gedan barai*

Move left foot forward, punch *chudan tsuki*

Move left foot to left

Block *gedan barai*

Move right foot forward, punch right *chudan tsuki*

Move left foot forward, punch left *chudan tsuki*

Move right foot forward, punching *chudan tsuki* and emitting loud *kiai*

Back turn with left foot

Block *gedan barai*

Move right foot forward,
punching *chudan tsuki*

Back turn with right foot

Block *gedan barai*

Move left foot forward,
punching *chudan tsuki*

Withdraw left foot

Return to *fudo dachi*

Pinan sono ichi, or 'the *kata* of peace and harmony', is the first of five *kata* that involve multiple attack and defence combinations. It also includes movements that may be copied, or duplicated, when using the *bo* (staff). Among techniques within the *pinan katas* are many defences against attacks with the *bo* as well as other weapons.

Assume *fudo dachi*

Raise hands to ears . . .

. . . before *yoi dachi*

Turn left 90° into *zenkutsu dachi*

Block *mae gedan barai*

Step forward, punching *chudan tsuki*

Move front foot to rear through 180°

Block *mae gedan barai*

Withdraw right foot

Adopt *neko ashi dachi* and strike *tettsui komi cami*

Move left foot forward, punching *chudan tsuki*

Turn left

Block *mae gedan barai*

Move right foot forward, blocking right *jodan uke*

Move left foot forward, blocking left *jodan uke*

Move right food forward, block right *jodan uke* and emit loud *kiai*

Cover groin with right fist, placing left fist to right ear, back turning with left foot.

Block gedan barai

Move right foot forward, punching chudan-tsuki

Cover groin with left fist, placing right fist to left ear, back turning with right foot.

Block right gedan barai

Move left foot forward, punching with chudan tsuki

Turn left, blocking left gedan barai

Move right foot forward, punching chudan tsuki

Move right foot forward, punching chudan tsuki

Move right foot forward, punching chudan tsuki and emitting loud kiai

Back turn half-step with left foot and prepare to block

Complete *shuto mawashi uke* and adopt *kokutsu dachi*

Move right foot forward at 45°, preparing for *shuto mawashi uke*

Complete *shuto mawashi uke*

Back turn half-step with right foot, preparing for *kokutsu dachi*

Complete *shuto mawashi uke*

turn left foot at 45° a half step, preparing to execute *shuto mawashi uke*

Complete *shuto mawashi uke*

Withdraw left foot in preparation . . .

. . . to resume *fudo dachi*

As its name suggests many of the techniques within *saifa* (rolling wave) *kata* are performed in circular movements that rely for ultimate effectiveness upon whip-like actions made between the elbow and wrist. One essential requirement when performing this *kata* is the perfection of *taisabaki* (body management) in order to be able to turn the hips efficiently and assist with the execution of various circular blocks and stances.

Assume *musubi dachi*

Raise hands to ears and move feet into *uchi hachiji dachi*

Assume *yoi dachi*

Move forward at 45°

Clasp right fist with left hand

Draw left foot to right, adopting *musubi dachi*

Move right fist to sternum and execute *hiji uke* (elbow block)

Move left foot back to *shiko dachi* while striking out in whip-like action

Move left foot forward at 45°

Draw right foot to left, adopting *musubi dachi*

Move left fist to sternum and execute *hiji uke*

Move right foot back into *shiko dachi* and strike with whip-like circular action *uraken shomen uchi*

Move forward at 45° and clasp right fist with left hand

Draw left foot to right, adopting *musubi dachi*

Move right fist to sternum and execute *hiji uke*

Move left foot back into *shiko dachi* while striking out with whip-like action

Move left foot up to right foot and slide it sideways to left to adopt long *kokotsu dachi*

Withdraw right foot up to left foot

Turn and face front, executing right *shuto gedan barai* and left *haito uchi uke*

Raise right knee into *hiza geri*

Continue momentum and immediately follow *hiza geri* and a *mae geri*

Step out to right and assume long *kokotsu dachi*

Withdraw left foot to right foot

Turn and face front, executing double block

Drive left knee up into *hiza geri*

Continue momentum and immediately follow *hiza geri* with *mae geri*

Step back into *zenkutsu dachi* and execute *morote haito uchi*

Withdraw both fists and . . .

. . . execute *jodan tsuki*

Move both hands in semi-circular actions outwards and downwards and execute a right *tettsui* strike against left palm

Bend back leg

Step across with right foot

Turn to rear and execute *morote haito uchi*

Withdraw both fists and . . .

. . . execute *morote tsuki jodan* followed by semi-circular movements to make a left *tettsui* strike

Raise right foot forward into *tsuriashi dachi* placing right fist behind head

Rotate 180° to your right and face front

Stamp right foot, using *sokuto*, at same time delivering *tettsui jodan uchi* and emitting loud *kiai*

Block with *kake uke*

Execute left *shita tsuki*

Raise left foot into *tsuriashi dachi* and place left fist behind head

Rotate 180° to your left

Execute *sokuto* to the floor while delivering left *tettsui jodan uchi*. Emit loud *kiai* followed by *kake uke*

Execute a right *shita tsuki*

Step forward right foot and deliver left *gyaku tsuki chudan*

Move through with left foot so feet are in line; withdraw left hand and cover lower area with right hand

Begin withdrawing right foot into *neko ashi dachi*

Execute a hook with the right hand and an inverted *nukite* thrust with the left hand

Complete *kaiten uke*

Withdraw hands in preparation for . . .

. . . thrust of left *jodan* and right *shotei morote uchi*

Withdraw right foot to left and place hands together above head

End with *musubi dachi*

Power Training

Many students ask if weight training, running and other forms of exercise will improve their Karate. The answer is that while many forms of alternative exercise can improve the level of fitness, there's nothing like Karate to improve Karate. It must be remembered that the fitness requirements of a long distance runner are totally different to those of a Karate exponent. All training must be relative to the needs of a *karate-ka*.

The training equipment reviewed here is used in all traditional Karate schools. Time is spent training students in its use and then time is spent utilizing the equipment. This has a much more direct affect on Karate skills than perhaps time spent on general physical improvement.

The punch bag

A Karate *dojo* is usually equipped with either a full two metre length punch bag, or a smaller half-body size version. Whichever, the bag should be stuffed with cloth, giving it a firm but yielding feel when touched. I've visited clubs where bags have been filled with sand and sawdust and before long they become compacted to resemble concrete-like lumps hanging from chains. At senior level, there are certain exercises that can be practised on these very hard bags, such as shin conditioning and heavy pushing techniques like *shotei*. The softer type is most suitable for general use.

Kin Ryoku Tanren
(Power Training)

The benefits of using a bag include the development of focus and judgement of distance. It also gives the *karate-ka* an opportunity to experience the 'feel' of sinking a full-strength blow or kick into a body as opposed to pulling short a technique, as the student would in *kumite*.

The striking post

The striking, or punching post, is called a *makiwari*. It is a tapered post, usully five feet in height above ground level and bolted firmly upright to the floor. Sometimes, an additional length is sunk into the floor itself. The post usually has two strike areas, the upper pad being just below the *karate-ka*'s shoulder level with the lower pad placed about knee height. All strikes may be practised on the post, but it is used primarily to strengthen the first two knuckles.

Whilst punching the *makiwari*, the body should remain relaxed. Showing no intention of real attack, the body rotates in accordance with

LEFT A student practices *tobi ushiro geri* (jumping back kick) on the training bag.

BELOW A *shuto yoko uchi* technique being strengthened against a *makawari* (striking post).

ABOVE *Chisi* (lever weight) being used to strengthen wrist and arm.

RIGHT Series of movements with *nigiri game* (weighted jars) develop a powerful grip.

the striking arm which is suddenly released with a whip-like action, simultaneous with an explosion of breath as the punch is delivered.

At first, the beginner will find that work on the *makiwari* will make the fists quite painful and to begin with, restricting the strikes to somewhere between twenty-five or fifty with each hand will provide a sufficient work-out. Gradually, the skin will harden and make it possible to strike up to five hundred times with each fist. The recognized pattern of *makiwari* practice is to make five hundred, or even a thousand, strikes with one hand one day, and then rest it the following day while repeating the exercise with the other hand.

Care should be taken to strike the *makiwari* with the first two knuckles, placing at least sixty per cent of the impact pressure upon the first knuckle. As the knuckles become conditioned, you can progress to striking equally with each knuckle. Do not allow the fist to bounce back off the *makiwari* after a strike. Follow through and hold the knuckles tight against the depressed pad for at least a second before slowly withdrawing the hand. This delayed withdrawal encourages the muscles which project as well as centre the punching technique. It also encourages the *karate-ka* to 'feel' not only the punch, but to be conscious of stance and position.

Although today we consider the *makiwari* as a striking post with pads of leather-covered rubber, the original Japanese form was of wood encased in a straw roll. The straw provided not only a striking surface, but was reputed also to possess antiseptic qualities beneficial to the bruised and chapped skin of the practitioners' fists.

As well as the upright *makiwari*, there is also a hanging *makiwari* made from either wood or a bunch of bamboo canes. Both are covered with straw padding. This suspended form of *makiwari* is used for practising certain hand or kicking techniques.

Some people use a wall-mounted *makiwari* made of sprung wood. Whilst these are useful for the development of certain strikes such as *shuto* (knife hand) or *uraken* (back fist), they are not recommended for practising punching techniques. The spring qualities of wall-mounted *makiwari* tend to deteriorate and punching a springless board can result in injury to the neck and upper back.

Lever weights

Lever weights are used primarily for the development of wrist and forearm strength, although the shoulder and *latissimus dorsi* muscles also derive benefit. They all become linked during the lever weight exercises which take on the form of rolling movements designed to develop the strength required for smooth, circular blocking techniques so common within *karate-do*.

Chisi, as these lever weights used by the Japanese are called, may be made quite easily by any handyman. They consist of a wooden pole handle of, say, half-a-metre in length, which is pushed through the bottom of a container, such as a good-sized paint tin, and bolted on the outside with a reinforced plate. The container is then filled with concrete, with the pole handle protruding. Obviously, these can be made to any size, the bigger the bulk and the longer the handle, the greater the initial strength required to use them.

Weighted jars

Beginner students are always surprised that training with anything so old-fashioned as weighted jars, or *nigiri-game* as the Japanese call them, can be effective in an age of highly modernized equipment. The fact is that grip strength, or finger strength, is often overlooked in training areas outside of the Martial Arts. I have had Karate students who have been heavily involved in weight training, some of whom were international power lifters, and yet they turned out to be sadly lacking when it came to grip or finger strength. This is probably because the grip strength in weight training is applied around a bar. Then, instead of gripping into anything, the power of the grip is applied solely to pulling.

The jars used may be of any earthenware type with a neck of the correct size for gripping with a span of the four fingers and thumb. It is best to work with two jars at any one time, as opposed to one on its own. Various exercise routines may be evolved with the necks of the jars gripped by their rims in the finger and thumb-tips of each hand. Once a twenty-minute period of movements can be performed, holding the jars in each hand by the finger and thumb-tips, the jars can be filled with a substance such as sand to increase the weight and thereby the gripping strength required.

The stone padlock

The original stone padlock, or *ishishasi*, used by the Japanese as a training implement, was said to have evolved from the types used on ancient doors. Others claim it may have come from the large hinges used on doors in the Far East. Nowadays, the *ishishasi*, or variances of it such as the kettle weight, are used to develop a wide range of blocking and punching techniques, as well as strong circular movements with the hands. Their use in exercise helps to develop back, chest and shoulder strength.

Iron clogs

Iron clogs, or *geta*, are worn to help develop hip and leg strength. Because the toes must grip the clogs tightly to avoid them slipping off, particularly while kicks are being practised, the wearing of *geta* also encourages control of the toes.

During my own training, I have found the wearing of *geta* beneficial when developing, say, the smooth and rhythmical line of the leg in a technique such as *mae keage* (straight pendulum kick). Repeated slow lifts of the knee, with the leg being gradually extended are extremely

1

ABOVE A pair of well-conditioned Karate hands holding *ishihashi*, the present day equivalent of an ancient Japanese stone padlock.

LEFT *Ishihashi* being used in *sanchin*, a type of training which develops the art of centreing an exponent's techniques.

2

ABOVE *Geta* used to practise *mae kaege*.

ABOVE RIGHT *Geta* in use to practise *hiza geri*.

OPPOSITE *Nukite* (finger tip strike) being thrust into a *tou* in order to develop stabbing power.

RIGHT One of a pair of heavy *geta* (iron clogs) worn to develop power in the hips and legs.

helpful. Alternatively, I would not encourage the wearing of heavy iron *geta* during the execution of, say, fast sharp kicks to the front and especially not in side leg raises.

The cane bundle

The cane bundle, or *tou*, is just that – a bundle of lightweight bamboo canes tightly bound together at top and bottom ends. It may be used for kicking at, to condition both shins and feet. It is especially useful for the strengthening of *nukite*, when straight fingers are thrust directly into the bundle and a single cane torn out from its core. This exercise develops tremendous finger strength.

The skipping rope

The skipping rope is an extremely useful fitness training aid because it helps with the development of hand and feet coordination. Start with periods of about twenty minutes of skipping, varying speeds as well as arm and leg movements. Then, relate this more to Karate in terms of time periods, skipping for spells of two or three minutes with one minute intervals. Vary this next, with fewer periods overall, but only thirty-second intervals.

General exercise procedures

In relation to Karate training, there is no need to exceed three-mile distances whilst running. I'd recommend one mile only, changing from jogging to sprinting to really striding out, every thirty yards or so. Help to preserve hip, knee and ankle joints by running wherever possible on soft ground. Always finish off after running with a series of muscle stretching exercises.

As a martial artist I have had the benefit of working directly with the National Coaching Foundation, a body liasing with the Sports Council to encourage the investigation of sports science and the various training methods required for each sport. These scientific procedures can help with fitness testing and the prescribing of programmes designed to counter weaknesses and improve an individual's performance. Obviously, everyone's needs differ, from the beginner to the international competitor at world level.

For those who seek individual help with a training programme and the development of their Karate performance, there is recourse to all manner of specialist publications, as well as access to various organizations such as the National Coaching Foundation, the English Karate Council and the British Karate Federation, and the courses they run. They all make splendid contributions to the improvement of standards.

Whilst sports science is extremely useful in aiding and improving a Karate athlete's performance, care must be taken not to become over-committed to sports and fitness training only. Many seem at first too anxious to try so many different methods, always looking for that which may provide the magic key. Yet, the general callisthenics and strength training used in Karate are specific and have lasted through time. They are tried and tested. The only additive required is the patience and diligence of the individual. There are no short cuts.

Jump rope being used for cardiovascular and reaction training.

Making Progress

When setting out to study Karate, it's both reassuring and important to know that your progress can be measured on a structured and regular basis. Whichever school you choose to join, it will doubtless have an established syllabus against which students are examined. This syllabus will be made up of pieces of practical and theoretical knowledge which you will be expected to master, and be able to perform, before progressing to a higher grade.

Beginner students passing through these cumulative stages of learning, beneath that of 1st Dan Black Belt, are called Kyu Grades and they wear differently-coloured belts to signify their *kyu*, or class. Early in the twentieth century, there were no grades at all in Karate with the exception of a teaching certificate sometimes formally referred to as the *menkyo kaiden* (certificate of advancement). Later, students simply joined in with a small group of Karate enthusiasts who worked and trained together under the watchful eye of a Master. After a number of years, the Master might consider a student to have made such progress that an Instructor's Certificate would be issued along with the coveted Black Belt and the rank of 1st Dan.

Jyotatsu

(Making Progress)

Nowadays, all schools of Karate have some sort or other of coloured belt system to signify student progress, but not all use identical colours for each stage of development. All of them, though, use the palest colours for lesser grades with belts becoming darker as progress is made towards the Black Belt.

Kyu *and* Dan *grades*

There are usually ten Kyu grades, ranging from the very beginner at 10th Kyu right through to 1st Kyu. Some schools may have interim grades and these are commonly signified by the wearing of coloured bands around the end of the belt, or even a special belt with a strip of separate colour running right through the centre of the belt lengthwise.

My own school, the United Kingdomo Seiki-Juku Karate Organisation, uses the following colours for Kyu Grades:

10th Kyu – *red belt*
9th Kyu – *blue belt*
8th Kyu – *purple belt with
        central white stripe*
7th Kyu – *purple belt*

6th Kyu – *yellow belt*

5th Kyu – *orange belt*
4th Kyu – *green belt with
        central white stripe*
3rd Kyu – *green belt*
2nd Kyu – *brown belt with
        central white stripe*
1st Kyu – *brown belt*

A young student steps forward to receive her spirit of Karate-do award from Sensei Perry.

Beyond the Kyu Grades come the Black Belt Dan Grades. The old-fashioned system additionally had the awards of *Doshi*, *Renshi*, *Kyoshi* and *Hanshi*. The exponent holding a Dan Grade would first demonstrate prowess as a fighter and competitor. When, in addition, his overall roundness of character was adjudged to be acceptable, a 1st Dan Grade might be given a *Doshi* award. In that case, the recipient would refer to himself as a 1st (or 2nd) Dan Doshi. The 3rd, 4th and sometimes 5th Dan Grades were given *Renshi* awards and 6th and 7th Dan the *Kyoshi* awards. The *Hanshi* award was reserved for 8th, 9th or 10th Dan Grades. The concept of these awards is Japanese and it is rare for them to be given in modern Karate. The principle does emphasize, though, the need for the combined assessment of both physical prowess and psychological make-up of any *karate-ka*'s performance and behaviour.

Widening circles of experience

An important difference between Japanese and European concept of Kyu Grades progress is recognized if you consider a student moving from, say, 10th Kyu to 9th Kyu. A European would consider this to be a step up the ladder for the 9th Kyu, making him superior to all 10th Kyu Grades.

Not so in the Japanese system, which shows the gradation of belts not as a ladder, but as a number of expanding circles. The innermost circle represents the 10th Kyu. The 9th Kyu is the next circle outside of that and the 8th Kyu circle surrounds that and so on, in circles spreading outwards to the 1st Kyu circle and then that of 1st Dan Black Belt. This symbolizes that students are graded according to their spreading experience as opposed to the building up of knowledge. Knowledge is academic and it is recognized that Karate is not academic, but physically inspired. Students are therefore measured primarily by physical ability born of experience, and as they spread outwards so do they encompass a responsibility for grades who have not yet progressed so far. It could be argued that this concept of training and development explains some of the differences between say, the management of Nissan and Ford.

Time spans between Kyu grading examinations may vary. Some schools grade students every three months. Others may work on the basis of a student being eligible for examination after having completed a period of, for example, twenty to thirty hours of training.

A period of six months to one year is the usual time stipulated before a 1st Kyu Brown Belt can be examined for progression to 1st Dan Black Belt status. The subsequent period before 2nd Dan consideration is usually two years, 3rd Dan three years after that, 4th Dan four years, and so on beyond that. Only the founder of a school (not a club) may hold a 10th Dan, though some founders consider themselves above 'grades' and don't claim any sort of Dan rating. A Karate Master is one who has attained the rank of 6th Dan, or above, and may be referred to as *Shihan*. A 6th Dan and above may wear a belt composed of red and white segments, or alternatively, a black belt with red and white bands running mid-way along its length.

Grading examinations

Despite what has been said about the co-development of both physical and psychological aspects, an instructor will not begin to look closely at the latter until a student begins to move towards the higher Kyu grades such as 2nd or 1st Kyu. Neither is fighting prowess a necessary consideration during the early stages because of the technical inefficiency of the students. Fighting prowess is usually encouraged later, otherwise students tend to discover one or two techniques with which they can defeat opponents and stick with these. This in itself restricts progress and prohibits them from experimenting and improving themselves. They hold on to what they've got, contrary to Karate's 'open hand' spirit which teaches one not to grasp and hold onto things, but to move through and search for new things, and thereby experience the true nature of *karate-do*.

When it comes to an actual grading examination, an instructor will usually call in an outside examiner to share in the assessment of students. Though the outsider will be able to assess each student with an open mind, consideration will be given to any intimate aspects of a candidate's profile the club instructor may provide and which may need to be taken into consideration. The grading syllabus itself is a set number of techniques laid down by a Martial Arts school and covers all that is felt important for students to learn at each particular stage of Kyu progress.

Whatever syllabus is adopted by a school, anything that has not been properly learned will show up during the pressure of a student's strict and formal examination and any weaknesses of imbalance of make-up will be exposed. I well remember when, at fourteen years of age, I had been graded quite highly while training with the UK national squad. On returning to my own *dojo*, others had informed my *sensei* that I was considered ready for further grading. I fought everyone in the club, each one in turn, without loss and including only one draw: yet I wasn't graded.

Three months later, I was given the same examination in the course of which I lost two fights and yet I was graded. My *sensei*'s explanation was that previously I had relied too much on strength and aggression with insufficient technical ability. This was possibly the outcome of the long period I'd previously spent involved with contest work. Whatever, my training was judged to have taken an unbalanced route, which had been corrected by the time of the second grading, when some technical quality was seen to have been restored to my performance. A hard lesson to learn at the age of fourteen.

Honorarium grades

One final comment about grades. In Japan, it is not unusual for someone who assists a Karate group, or even a single *dojo*, in some financial or other way to be given an honorary grade. This system was extended into the UK in the 1960s by the Japanese teachers ready to show their appreciation to those who had helped establish Karate in their new adopted homeland. Unfortunately, these honorary grades were abused by certain English instructors who went away with them to open clubs of their own, claiming full status as 3rd or 4th Dans.

This would never have happened in Japan, where it would have been considered a very dishonourable act. To achieve an honorary grade requires no physical work or mental training, though it is a fine recognition when made in good faith to a worthy candidate. Under normal circumstances, the only grades that exist within the pattern of *karate-do* are those which have been hard-earned and fought for. These are the true grades by which progress is measured.

Karate for Children

In the early 1960s it was unusual for any Karate club to take junior members. Today, many enrol children from six years of age upwards and together these youngsters form a substantial percentage of students in the UK. Their standard of Karate is generally good, depending upon their teacher or school, and can be quite amazing. I have twelve-year-olds in my own club who have advanced to quite high grades. While being excellent in form, some of their techniques are delivered with a power that would easily floor an adult attacker. But, despite their explosive potential as Martial Arts exponents, the subject of children in Karate is one deserving of the greatest care and attention. It is in today's children that the future of Karate exists and it is every teacher's job to make sure they are properly nurtured.

Teaching children is one of the most important tasks in any teacher's workload. Only the best instructors in a club should be in charge of junior sessions. There is so much to be considered, so much to be preserved. Despite a general realization of all this, too many teachers still set about trying to teach senior Karate to juniors.

It must be remembered that Karate in its original form was designed as a pure fighting art in an age when people did not live to advanced years. There was no need for training routines to take into account any long-term effect of stress on joints and such complications as osteo-arthritis. Children today should be kept well clear of anything of that nature. They grow in fits and starts at different times and can do without extra stress which may have an adverse effect on their muscular and skeletal structure.

Kodomo
(Karate for Children)

Dangers and limitations

Although children are very supple, due to incomplete muscular development, their joints may become hyper-mobile. Therefore, to help avoid osteo-arthritis in later life, it is important that, along with stretching to stimulate suppleness, there are also given strengthening exercises to build up muscle round the joints and give them 'integrity'.

Hand conditioning for juniors is strictly a 'no-go' area. The bones in their young hands, and most especially those of the wrist, are underdeveloped. Things such as push-ups on the knuckles, or any exercise causing jarring or trauma to any joint, should be avoided. So should any exercise that may impair the development of any bones or cause joints to become hyper-mobile.

RIGHT A children's class in *seiza*, prior to exchanging salutations.

BELOW A youngster attempts to focus a *mawashi geri* to his partner's hand.

BELOW RIGHT Sensei Perry's own children, son Scott (left) and daughter Carly, are among his younger students.

1

2

3

Turning from the physical, the teacher must also bear in mind the psychological differences between his senior and junior students. Juniors generally lack the ability to concentrate for long periods or to endure sustained intensive pressure training. Children have physical limitations and, of course, their emotional immaturity has to be considered.

Karate is an exceptional form of self-defence and one of the fastest to be learned. However, instructors must realise that the techniques they teach to children should be slightly watered down so that they cannot be used to inflict injury in playground scuffles. The emotional immaturity of children prohibits them from showing the control you would expect from a senior if being teased or goaded into a fight situation outside of the *dojo*. A good instructor, then, will offer junior students techniques which are safe for children within the club and for their friends outside the *dojo*, who may not train in Karate.

Competition Karate for children

Competitions are arranged for children from the age of six and upwards. These are very much 'fun' events for the younger ones, with little pressure being imposed upon them, and certainly no coaching from the sidelines by either parents or instructors. I always feel that everyone who makes the effort to go to a competition should be rewarded with something in some way or another — a small medal, trophy, token or certificate. My policy is that no competition of any serious nature should be entered by children until they are at least fourteen years old.

Some children reach junior Black Belt by the age of fourteen, but it is unusual for a junior to achieve this level any younger. Apart from the physical aspect of their Karate performance, it's incredible how a youngster who may not be doing so well at school, is able to pick up and remember quite a range of Japanese words and their meanings.

Within competitions held only for those of twelve years of age and over, there are weight divisions, and also height categories for entrants. This is to prevent a boy who is maybe only five feet tall, but weighing seventy kilos, meeting a boy of the same weight but standing six feet two inches. The taller boy's limbs and joints would not be able to sustain the strain and punishment to the same extent as his shorter opponent.

All things considered, Karate is good for children and children will be good for Karate. They have much to gain from Karate; in being able to defend themselves they gain a greater self-confidence, supported by self-control and discipline. And from children, Karate will get the *karate-ka* seniors of tomorrow. Meanwhile, they deserve the best we have available.

ABOVE LEFT A young student developing focus and power for kicks by striking at a focus pad held by her instructor.

LEFT A group of young students don protective equipment before free sparring.

ABOVE A children's class do their push-ups from flat hands.

YOUNG STUDENTS Young students practise *yakusoku kumite* (pre-arranged sparring).

Karate for Women

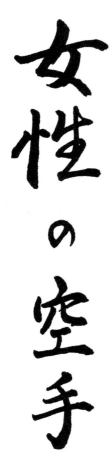

女性の空手

Jyosei-no-Karate

(Karate for Women)

When Karate was first introduced into the UK, the Japanese instructors of the day didn't consider it to be something suitable for practice by women and they were excluded. However, during the past fifteen years, men and women have been commonly sharing mixed classes throughout Europe. Even in Japan, women now practise Karate. Women have shown that they are quite able to grasp the fundamentals of Karate. What they may lack in power, compared to a man of equal size, they are able to make up for in speed and technique and thereby become quite capable of felling an opponent or breaking solid objects.

My own view has always been that women competing in Judo, for instance, are not given the best of opportunities to exploit all of their natural physical qualities whilst grappling on the mat.

Karate is full of free-flowing movements and graceful techniques which have to be performed at all times. These provide an opportunity for an almost balletic display of female strength, especially when performing in the *kata* sections of competitions, when women are able to compete against men at the highest levels. There are also, of course, separate groups for women in *kata* competitions as well as team *kata* and contest *kumite* events.

One important aspect which any woman, as well as her instructor, need to bear in mind is the physiological difference between herself and a male. Because of the difference in the shape of the male and female hip, there is a tendency for some women to be knock-kneed. This causes a weakness in one of the quadricep muscles surrounding the knee joint which, unless corrected or protected from strain, may lead to cartilage trouble or even osteo-arthritis at some later date.

A safeguard against this happening is a substantial amount of training in order to condition these quadriceps. Fortunately, the warming-up exercises within a Karate class, along with stance training, will help these muscles to develop and gain more strength to meet with the strain that the practice of Karate will place upon the knee they are supporting.

Additionally, women in Karate generally should embark upon a specific training routine for this particular muscle group – one-legged squats performed to no more than a ninety degree drop on the supporting leg, or specific exercises performed in a weight training gym, will do much to strengthen the quadricep muscles.

Protective equipment is worn by women during contests. The wearing of head guards, plastic breast protectors, gum shields as well as shin, foot and arm protectors is recommended.

LEFT A Kyu Grade woman student practises *kanzetsu geri* (joint dislocation kick).

BELOW Sensei Perry leads a class in *kata*.

RIGHT A Kyu Grade student attempts *ushiro mawashi geri* during *kumite*.

BELOW A Black Belt student free-sparring with a Bu'sen Black Belt instructor.

ABOVE A student practises self-defence with a senior Dan Grade.

LEFT A more realistic self-defence situation in which a student demonstrates *kakato geri* (heel kick) against an aggressor's throat. While high heels are generally regarded as a hindrance in an attack situation, they can be applied to good effect.

Kumite

Kumite
(Sparring)

Kumite (sparring) can be split into two groups, simple *kumite* in which partners spar freely with each other and *yakusoku kumite* (pre-arranged sparring). *Yakusoku kumite* is the application, by cooperating partners, of clearly-defined groups of attacking and defensive techniques. These repeatedly rehearsed sparring movements are designed to improve *hyoshi* (timing), *chosi* (rhythm) and *mai-ai* (judgement of fighting distance).

Yakusoku kumite itself can be divided into three areas. These are referred to as *ippon kumite*, *sambon kumite* and *gohon kumite*. During *ippon kumite*, one partner delivers a pre-determined attacking technique while the other blocks or counters in various stances. *Sambon kumite*, sometimes referred to as 'three-step pre-arranged sparring', is a little more advanced, as the attacking partner throws three pre-determined attacking techniques to be either blocked or countered by the defender. The three attacks may be to the upper, middle or lower level of the defendant's body. They may be all punching techniques, or a mixture of strikes and kicks. Finally, *gohon kumite* is performed similarly, but with a selection of five pre-determined techniques.

Although *yakusoku kumite* may be a lower grade's first introduction to sparring in the *dojo*, it is something which remains part of every *karate-ka*'s regular training routine right through the senior ranks, including Dan grades.

Working with a partner

Because they are working with a cooperating partner, it is natural that many who train in *yokusoku kumite* are careful not to inflict any real injury. But they may finish up delivering attacks with little resolve or impact. The performance then becomes purely aesthetic and bears no relationship to real combat situations. At worst, it can degenerate into no more than a game, and the whole routine becomes of little value.

It is therefore more beneficial for anyone starting out with *yokusoku kumite* training to work with a partner of a higher grade. Such a partner will have the experience and control to tone down powerful deliveries so that, while they do not cause injury, they remain strong and positive attacks. In turn, the defender will be forced to respond with equally positive defensive techniques and the whole routine becomes meaningful.

Variations of *yakusoku kumite* routines may be introduced into either

ippon, sambon or *gahon kumite.* In *gohon kumite,* for instance, a partner may call for one specific technique (say, a front kick to the stomach) to be repeated five times in succession, each time relying on the opposing partner to move back and defend. Similarly, some may choose to introduce combinations of one sort or another into *sambon kumite.*

Ippon kumite, the one-point sparring form, may be practised by a partner naming a single technique but continuing for some minutes if necessary to try to use it against the defender, who is continually blocking and changing free-moving stances.

Some instructors may choose to select a student to stand in front of perhaps a dozen higher grades. Each in turn will be allowed to throw one or more pre-arranged techniques at the student who is thereby made to stretch all blocking and countering skills to the limit. The student, incidentally, should be standing with his rear foot firmly on the floor against a wall. This ensures he can move only sideways, showing good *taisabaki* (body management) in order to help deflect and counter-attack his partner's techniques.

Free sparring

Free sparring should not be encouraged until a student has a firm grasp of the basics of Karate and achieved a high level of fitness. Whereas *kata* sets a strict discipline of formal exercises to which the student must adhere, sparring enables the student to introduce his or her own personality. It's often possible to grasp students' character make-up by watching how they perform when free-sparring.

It is generally accepted that attacking techniques to the groin, knee, throat and eye are not used in free sparring in the *dojo*. However, this may not always be the case, so upon visiting any club it's advisable to check on its particular rules before involving yourself in a sparring session. While some schools treat *dojo*-sparring primarily as a method of improving techniques, others may encourage it as a free-fighting occasion in which injury can occur. This can happen in the UK and is certainly not unusual in Japan.

There must always remain a clear dividing line between contest fighting and *dojo* sparring with a partner in a club environment. Within a club, the emphasis should be upon the *karate-ka* being able to spar in an atmosphere which, while being competitive, is also supportive. In such an environment, he or she will be encouraged to experiment with their whole repertoire of techniques.

Students in schools which decree club *dojo*-sparring should be approached in the same manner as contest work are actually missing out on developing a full range of techniques. They will tend to stick with the techniques they've found to be contest-winners and ignore the rest of the syllabus. It must also be remembered that a *karate-ka* who becomes too used to contest sparring always performs according to contest rules in which attacks to the groin, knees and other vulnerable parts are prohibited. Simulated attacks to these prohibited areas are

A young Dan Grade attacks
with a punch to her
opponent's head . . .

. . . and later steps in to deliver
a powerful chopping heel kick
to his collar bone.

still encouraged in *dojo*-sparring between selected students, although usually at not lower than Black Belt standard.

Attitudes to winning

Even with all these points in favour of *dojo*-sparring as opposed to contest or competition sparring, there are still critics who claim it is no more than a game and therefore of no use in a real fight situation. However, any idea of maiming and emerging always as the victor is a complete nonsense and an objective that only a very junior Karate student would consider. It is always said that never losing does not necessarily mean always winning, and when a student comes to understand this, it's an indication of progress from the beginners' class to senior levels.

The real essence of any sort of sparring is not the consideration of strong man, weak man, of strong technique, weak technique, or of the victor and the vanquished. It is the consideration of mutual cooperation between two combatants, striving and giving of their best to increase their own and each other's skills and understanding. That is *karate ne senti nashi!*

Karate ne senti nashi can be more easily understood when a *karate-ka* has engaged in enough contest, combat or serious *dojo*-sparring situations to appreciate that neither combatant can be a solely defensive or offensive person. Each must learn to move in harmony with the other in order to search out openings and weaknesses in the opponent's make-up. Once able to compete in this manner, it becomes more easy to understand the meaning of *karate ne senti nashi*.

It is easy to become too confident from winning, or to feel ashamed about losing, but these reactions are out of step with the philosophy of Karate. In sparring or contest work, you must regard the delivery to you of a powerful, well-timed scoring technique from an opponent as something which presents you with a movement to be later studied and analyzed. How was it executed? Why didn't you counter successfully? Were you concentrating enough? Were you wrongly positioned? What can you learn from it? In the same way, the highlights of your own techniques provide lessons for your opponent or partner.

In Japan, it is generally acknowledged that when sparring in *kumite* in preparation for real combat or contest work, the mind of the *karate-ka* must remain calm but alert. Personal ego is abandoned and the mind concentrates solely upon the technical aspects of *kumite*, otherwise the learning rate will be slowed.

Approaching kumite

It's during *kumite* that you test not only technical skills, but also correct breathing, relaxed but controlled stances, and the correct use of *kiai*. You must first control your breathing prior to the start of a contest. Then, during combat, it is important to conceal your breathing pattern from your opponent as he may be able to forecast your attack from it.

ABOVE Male and female students compete.

LEFT Sensei Perry counters a student's attack.

RIGHT A young boy student takes on his instructor.

A jamming *mae geri* to the chin

ABOVE Hook kick to the jaw...

... and a disabling knee attack.

Your opponent will sense your forthcoming explosion of breath, coinciding with your *kiai*, and be able to block or counter in order to foil your attack.

Develop also the proper way of looking at your opponent during *kumite*. Look towards him at eye level. Look into his eyes, but not with a fixed stare. Remain open-eyed, with full surrounding filter-vision providing a complete view of your opponent and of the movement of his limbs, giving early warning of impending attacking techniques such as round-house blows or kicks. Avoid a fixed stare which concentrates upon his eyes alone, particularly at moments when you're put under pressure. Your filter-vision will narrow and you won't see the round-house attacks coming. So, maintain a relaxed look at all times, just as if you were looking out through a window with no exactness or intensity.

This form of 'relaxed looking' is another technique that may be practised in *seiza*. Instead of half-closing the eyes as in *seiza* normally, hold them open and look towards a candle positioned, say, about three to six metres away from you. Practice periods of looking at the candle without blinking. Begin with a period of two minutes, working up to about twenty minutes, avoiding at all times the narrowing of your filter-vision as you're tempted to drift off into a fixed stare.

Contest Karate

Competition Karate is now an established sport, with events held regularly in many countries under recognized rules and regulations. WUKO (the World Union of Karate Organizations) is the international governing body in control of World Championships. There are both *kumite* (free fighting) and *kata* (pre-arranged forms of movement) competitions.

Kumite is probably the competition most familiar to the general public as it appears to the uninitiated to be the most visually exciting and for that reason receives media exposure. *Kumite* provides the *karata-ka* with an opportunity to assemble hard-earned skills, reflexes, breathing, fitness, stamina and techniques, and apply them against an opponent in a combat situation. Short of a street mugging, or other incident in which a *karate-ka* may be called upon to defend him or herself outside of the *dojo*, *kumite* is probably the nearest any of them will ever get towards experiencing real combat and the true spirit of Karate. *Kumite* also stimulates the *bushido* (non-quitting spirit) and emphasizes the importance of remaining controlled and concentrated under pressure at all times.

Win or lose, a *karate-ka* can do no better than come out of a contest having given of his or her personal best. This will have contributed to their personal growth. Simultaneously, they will have provoked and encouraged their opponent to act and react to their maximum potential and thereby contributed to their growth also. Together they will have each acquired and exchanged mutual benefits. That is ideally what Karate is all about, rather than the colour of medal hanging from the neck.

Shi-ai
(Contest Karate)

The rules of kumite

A Karate contest, or match as they are sometimes called, takes the form of *kumite* between two opponents. They are controlled by a referee and a 'shadow' referee who both move around the mat attempting to observe the fighters from all angles at all times. An adjudicator sits outside the contest area where there is also placed a table at which sit a timekeeper and a recorder. The contest area measures eight-by-eight metres and points are awarded in favour of either opponent delivering a scoring technique while he or she is within that area. However, if either scores while the other steps out of the area, 'Stop!' is called by the referee and a score awarded to the successful attacker in the normal manner.

All the referee's commands to contestants, and the award of points or penalties, are called out as they occur and underlined by a comprehensive range of hand and arm signals to the recorder and timekeeper's table. Scores are displayed on scoreboards on the officials' table or on giant scoreboards which are sometimes avilable at large tournaments. Once a contest begins, legal scoring areas are strikes to the face, neck, chest, body, stomach and the back. Strikes or attempted strikes to the knee or groin are disallowed. Excessive facial contact is prohibited, but the referee will consider if the contestant who was struck in the face had actually advanced into the technique and therefore contributed to the incident.

Currently, the maximum score in a contest is three full points or six half-points. A full point would be awarded for a technique judged to be so correct in timing and power as well as form, that it would have struck with maximum effect if delivered without any control on the part of the attacker. These full-point techniques are strikes which, if not pulled but delivered with maximum force, would cause considerable injury to the recipient.

Half-points are awarded for techniques judged to be anything less than worthy of a full point, but they should fulfil at least two of the three criteria of a full point technique. Penalties are given for prohibited behaviour. They are imposed by the referee calling 'Stop!' and delivering a verbal warning or a half-point penalty to the offender for a minor or serious infringement respectively. A full-point penalty is awarded for a more serious infringement. For a very serious breach of the rules, there can be disqualification from the match or even eviction from the complete tournament.

Competition time is of three minutes duration for all senior matches and two minutes for women and junior contests. A series of time extensions may be given if there is no conclusive result at or before the end of normal time. Usually, no more than three extra-time periods are awarded. At some tournaments, if a draw still remains after time extensions, a 'first kill' contest is held in which the first person to score during a further extension is declared the winner.

Contest rules and regulations are forever being up-dated and improved upon, so the above is no more than a broad summary of how a match is fought and scored. For a greater understanding you should acquire a W.U.K.O. rule book. Study this carefully and then watch a few tournaments and see how the rules are interpreted and applied by the officials.

As in most Martial Art forms, things can happen in Karate so quickly and often in such a skilled and subtle manner, that a technique is often performed and completed before the lay spectator is aware that anything has taken place. There is no comprehension as to why, when, or how a point has been scored.

Contact Karate competitions

Various associations have tried to apply different rules and methods of competition in attempts to make Karate more of a spectator sport. As a

Two young Black Belts seen here
battling for an *ippon* (full point)
during a hard-fought contest.

result, 'all-contact' events were introduced, allowing full contact blows to the body and kicks to the head, but still disallowing punches to the head. There have also been so-called 'contact-karate' events in which combatants wear gloves. These bouts tend to simulate boxing except that a number of kicks are permitted, although leg attacks and sweeps are not allowed. Despite my own reservations about these types of Karate competition, it cannot be denied that they appeal to young or athletic Karate students. They encourage competitively-minded students to hone techniques and work on them extra hard primarily for the purpose of winning contests. So, in this way at least Competition Karate helps to improve skills.

However, I consider that most of the forms of so-called 'contact' Karate which have been introduced, should find a new name for themselves which does not include the word 'Karate'. Their violence deters parents and prospective students and does nothing to promote either the spirit or the image of Karate.

To exhibit and experience the true essence of combative Karate, there would have to be contests in which nothing was barred, including joint dislocation, bone-breaking and killing techniques. Each contestant would need to commit themselves to absorbing bodily punishment in order to deliver disabling counters. In fact, the only 'true' Karate competition would be to put two Karate fighters in a room, lock them in and wait for one of them to knock on the door to be let out.

While that's not what any of us want to happen in this day and age, anything less in competitive terms can only be regarded as superficial and do nothing to further the interests of true Karate. Nevertheless, most students who go through a phase of wanting to show their prowess in competitions eventually settle down and generally get back to studying Karate for what I consider the correct reasons.

Some degree of competitive element must always, though, be within each *karate-ka*. As I pointed out in the Introduction to this book, Karate is competitive in as much as you are for ever in competition with your own self. This is typified in the performance of *kata*.

Kata is also introduced at competitive level, with competitions for the individual as well as team events. If these competitions help to get youngsters to practise and to take *kata* more seriously, they can only be for the good.

The Study of Weapons

In recounting the history of Karate it was explained how agricultural and domestic implements came into use as fighting weapons in Okinawa during the late 1400s. At first, skills with these sort of weapons became known as *Kobu-jutsu*, but this was later changed to *Kobu-do*, placing the emphasis upon the physical and spiritual as in *karate-do*.

Some schools in modern day Karate teach *Kobu-do*, although it is generally confined to those grades of 1st Dan Black Belt and above. I would never teach *Kobu-do* to any student under the age of eighteen. Even then, selection for *Kobu-do* training is not an automatic procedure. More often than not, a candidate will ask for training and the student's instructor must decide whether or not he or she is a suitable candidate. On the other hand, there are a relatively few schools teaching *Kobu-do* only, with no Karate involvement.

The *Kobu-do* student has to bear in mind the laws of the land pertaining to the carrying of offensive weapons when, however innocently, equipment is being transported around. The UK's regulations can be slightly vague when dealing with cases involving weapons other than flick-knives and firearms; the police must prove that a person caught carrying a weapon is doing so 'with intent' in order to obtain a conviction. However the best way to avoid any misunderstandings, harassments or embarrassments is for *Kobu-do* students to store their weapons in a safe place at their Karate club. Failing that, make sure your weapons are in a suitable case at the bottom of your training bag if they must be carried around. Never carry them on public transport.

The basic principles and techniques practised by the *Kobu-do* student are the same as those applied in Karate. The difference is that in *Kobu-do* the students have to grasp weapons and learn to regard and use them as natural extensions to the body. They are able, when necessary, to fight at a longer range from their opponent.

The principles of *Kobu-do* can also have an application in self-defence, if you imagine substituting, say, a modern walking stick or umbrella for one of the standard weapons. Conversely, the Karate student who studies *Kobu-do* gains a valuable understanding of the types of attack he must be prepared to counter with his bare hands if ever faced with an armed opponent. *Kobu-do* also provides the Karate student with a better judgement of distance, helps build up good reflexes and reactions and at the very least offers an introduction into another area of Martial Arts interest.

Buki No Gaku Shu
(Study of weapons)

There are many sorts of weapons used in *Kobu-do* practice in different schools. Those featured below are the five in most common use. All are used in various open *kata* competitions, but not in the World Union of Karate *kata* competitions.

The bo (staff)

The *bo* measures approximately two metres in length and is made of polished hardwood. It sometimes tapers from the centre towards each end. The finest *bo* is made not from a branch, but is hewn from the centre core of a whole tree trunk. This ensures it is free from knots and weaknesses and provides such strength that a skilled exponent can smash a sword blade in half with a single stroke of the *bo*.

The *bo* is usually the first weapon taught in *Kobu-do* because its movements relate generally to the teaching of *mai-ai* (fighting distance), so essential in the use of all weapons. Whereas Karate training puts importance on stance and strength, *Kobu-do* places more emphasis on the application of speed and the centreing of the weapon's delivery.

As well as being used for striking, the *bo* can be thrust into an opponent's body, or used to apply leverage against the joints and also to throw an opponent. The length of the weapon provides it with certain advantages over the sword, and a well-applied strike to an opponent's head will almost certainly prove fatal.

The kama (sickle)

The *kama* still remains a legitimate farming implement – it is said to be commonly used for killing the Okinawa viper. The *kama* is used in single and cross-blocking techniques and when reversed it becomes an awesome weapon for close-range fighting.

The sai (truncheon)

The *sai* is used in Karate schools because, apart from use as a weapon, practice with it helps to develop hand and wrist strength. The *sai* is said to have evolved from the sword held in the Great Hand of Indra, a Hindu god incorporated into Buddhism as a protective deity.

Modern versions of the *sai* often have a brightly chromed appearance, but earlier types, and certainly the originals, were forged of one piece of metal for added strength. They were brownish in colour. An advantage of the *sai* is that it can be used with the same movements as in all the standard blocks and attacks in Karate. Also, an attack with a sword may be rendered useless by trapping its blade in one of the smaller tines.

The tonfa (rice grinder)

The *tonfa* is an interesting weapon because, even with very basic Karate training, it can be used to fit perfectly into the movements of all the

The fluid and powerful through-movement of the *bo* (staff).

blocks, elbow thrusts and sideways strikes. It can also be spun for use in different directions. A version of the *tonfa* has been adopted by the USA police forces as well as various other control and armed forces throughout the world. It has been found more effective than the orthodox truncheon as it can be used to restrain, lock and control, as well as to strike.

The nunchaku (*rice flail*)

The batons of the original *nunchaku* were made of a very dense wood and shaped to a round cross-section. They were linked by a metal ring and sometimes a third baton was added to the flail. Later, they were made with octagonal cross sections, it being believed that a strike from such a shape inflicted more surface damage than would a smooth, rounded surface. *Tonfa* and *bo* are sometimes made with similar octagonal cross-sections. It was the popularity of Martial Arts films during the early 1970s that awoke Western interest in the *nunchaku*.

The *nunchaku* can be used in a variety of ways. The simplest is to hold the batons together in one hand and use them as a club. They have greater power and manoeuvrability when being swung round to make a strike, due to the generation of centrifugal force. The *nunchaku* may also be used as an effective garrotte around an opponent's neck, or in a pincer-type manner against various joints. Because the exponent can use the *nunchaku* in either hand, or with both, and can launch attacks with it from so many angles, it has to be considered the most versatile of weapons.

ABOVE RIGHT Wearing traditional black *hakama*, Sensei Perry demonstrates use of the *kama* against a sword attack.

ABOVE FAR RIGHT Fighting stance with a pair of *sai*.

RIGHT *Tonfa* being used in *kata*.

FAR RIGHT Both bars of the *nunchaku* can be seen here during weapon practice.

Tameshiwari

試し割り

Tameshiwari
(Destruction)

A display of *tameshiwari* (destruction) is a true and excellent way of testing the spirit and power of a *karate-ka* and, because it so captures the public's imagination, it is often the focal point of a Karate demonstration. Apart from the spectacle of *tameshiwari*, everyone can relate to the pain of punching knuckles into a brick which may or may not break.

In fact, given time and a little knowledge and guidance, many people not connected with Karate could become proficient at breaking hard objects with their bare hands. This ability, itself, has nothing to do with Karate as such. It is simply a way to test-bed our techniques, a way of finding out just how much destructive power has been built up within them. The importance of *tameshiwari* is particularly apparent in schools where strikes to the body, face and head are continually controlled. The student always has a nagging doubt about the full effectiveness of a technique – would the blows really work against a real-life attacker? *Tameshiwari* dispels these doubts since if students are able to smash through two inches of wood with a straight punch, then it may be assumed they'd break a rib or collar bone quite easily. This gives them the necessary assurance and avoids the need to experiment on fellow students!

In *tameshiwari*, the most important thing is the mental attitude of the *karate-ka* attempting the break. He or she must perceive it to be simply the normal performance of a much practised technique, but one which on this occasion they extend and follow right through. Whatever is being broken just happens to have been in the way of the punch, kick or whatever the technique employed. It has a *zen-like* simplicity.

Any of the natural weapons we possess may be used to strike, except perhaps the middle finger joint at the back of the hand. This carries a tendon which can be severely injured if too much force is applied.

The photographs in this chapter show a number of my senior students executing impressive breaks in the course of testing the power of their techniques – punches, kicks and blows from the elbow and shin.

Preparing for tameshiwari

Some schools begin *tameshiwari* quite early in a student's Karate career, but I avoid this because much time needs to be devoted to conditioning exercises before breaking is attempted. *Tameshiwari* should not be introduced until a student has completed three of four years general practice. Then, it may be practised by both men and women, but only under careful supervision. No-one under eighteen years of age should be encouraged or allowed to practise *tameshiwari*.

Some modern schools of Karate take the view that *tameshiwari* is no longer necessary and neither is hand-conditioning, since the *karate-ka* no longer has to fight people who wear armour. There is no need to be able to destroy armour or heavy protective clothing in order to fell an opponent. This is a poor argument. You have only to consider a natural fist to realize that it is ill-equipped to deliver strong blows into something as hard as the human head. The fist has no natural padding or protection to the knuckles other than a thin layer of skin.

So, I strongly assert that conditioned knuckles are much safer and efficient than knuckles which are not conditioned, in either a fight in a *dojo* situation or in real combat. However, I recommend the *karate-ka* to consider and take action upon the following points before attempting *tameshiwari*:

● Can the area of your body being used to break with, be conditioned?

● What might the medical implications or outcome be as a result of any conditioning?

● How long will the conditioning take to become effective?

In earlier chapters dealing with hand techniques some steps that can be taken to condition and preserve hands have been outlined. For more detailed and comprehensive information and guidance about all protective conditioning, you should consult your instructor before embarking upon the study of *tameshiwari*.

BELOW LEFT
Breaking concrete tiles with the elbow.

Breaking concrete blocks with a knife hand strike.

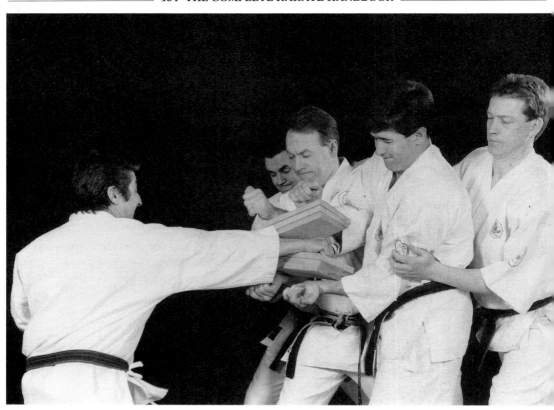

FAR LEFT Three one-inch thick boards are supported by students while being broken with a punch.

BELOW LEFT Fellow students support three one-inch boards as they're broken by *ushiro mawashi geri*.

LEFT A baseball bat supported behind the legs of two students is broken with a shin kick.

BELOW A striking knife hand breaks two one-inch boards supported by students.

The Language of Karate

Japanese is the universal language of Karate and your life in the *dojo* will become all the more relaxed and enjoyable once you begin to understand what more experienced *karate-ka* are talking about. However, most Europeans find Japanese words difficult to pronounce, so for all the words listed I've provided some phonetic guidance. Practise saying these words — and listen to others using them.

Seiki Juku

(True Spirit School)

ago tsuki	a-go-ski	jaw thrust
atama	at-a-ma	head
bo	boe-o	staff
bushido	boo-she-doe	fighting spirit
chisi	chee-see	lever weights
chosi	cho-see	rhythm
chudan tsuki	choo-dan ski	middle thrust
chusoku	choo-sock-oo	ball of foot
dachi	da-she	stance
dan	dan	Black Belt grade
doshi	dosh-ee	teacher level
fudo dachi	foo-doe dash-ee	formal stance
gedan barai	gee-dan bal-eye	downward parry
geta	ge-tta	iron clogs
gohon kumite	go-hon kum-ettay	sparring with five pre-determined techniques
haisoku	high-sock-oo	instep
haito jodan uchi	high-toe jaw-dan oo-chi	ridge hand upper strike
haito uchi uke	high-toe oo-chi oo-kay	ridge hand outside block
hakama	ha-kamma	traditional split skirt
hanshi	han-she	Master of Karate
hara	ha-la	lower stomach
heisoku dachi	high-sock-oo dash-ee	closed stance
hijiate	hijji-attay	elbow strike
hijiate age	hijji-attay ag-ay	rising elbow strike
hijiate jodan	hijji-attay jaw-dan	upper elbow strike
hiji uke	hijji oo-kay	elbow block
haito	high-toe	inner knife hand

hiza	he-za	knee
hiza geri	he-za gelli	knee kick
hyoshi	high-or-she	timing
ipponken	ee-pon-ken	middle knuckle fist
ippon kumite	ee-pon kum-ettay	sparring with one single technique
ipponken uchi jodan	ee-pon-ken oo-chi jaw-dan	middle knuckle strike to upper area
ishishasi	i-she-ha-she	stone padlock
jodan tsuki	jor-dan ski	upper thrust
jodan uke	jor-dan oo-kay	upper block
kaiten uke	ki-ten oo-kay	circular or rolling block
kakato	ka-ka-toe	heel
kakato geri	ka-ka-toe gelli	heel kick
kake dachi	ka-ki da-she	hook stance
kama	ka-ma	sickle
kamiza	ka-me-za	focal point of dojo
kanzetsu geri	kan-set-su gelli	joint kick
kata	ka-ta	form, shape or related group of exercises
katana	ka-tan-a	sword
kake uke	ka-kay oo-kay	hook block
karate	ka-la-tay	empty hand
karate-do	ka-la-tay-doe	philosophy, or way of karate
karate-gi	ka-la-tay-gee	karate suit
karate-ka	ka-la-tay-ka	student of Karate
keiko	kay-coe	chicken beak
keiko uchi	kay-coe oo-chi	chicken beak strike
kiai	kee-eye	spirit shout
kiba dachi	kee-ba da-she	straddle stance
kin geri	kin gelli	groin kick
kinhin	kin-hin	controlled breathing whilst moving
kihon	kee-hon	practice of basics
kobu-do	ko-bu-doe	skill or way with weapons
koken	ko-ken	wrist
koken uchi	ko-ken oo-chi	wrist strike
koken jodan uke	ko-ken or-dan oo-kay	wrist block
kokutsu dachi	ko-cot-soo da-she	back leaning stance
kumite	kum-ettay	free sparring
Kyoshi	ki-oshi	teacher of high attainment
mai-ai	my-eye	judgement of fighting distance
mae gedan barai	my gee-dan bal-eye	downward parry
mae geri	my gelli	front kick

mae kakato geri	my ka-ka-toe gelli	front heel kick
mae keage	my key-ag-ay	front pendulum kick
makiwari	ma kee-wal-i	strike or punching post
mawashi geri	ma-washee gelli	roundhouse kick
menkyo kaiden	men-kee-o ki-eedan	certificate of advancement
moroachi dachi	mo-roshee da-she	one-step stance
morote haito uchi	mo-rot-ay high-toe oo-chi	double right hand strike
morote tsuki	mo-rot-ay ski	double thrust
morote tsuki chudan	mo-rot-ay ski choo-dan	double thrust to middle area
musubi dachi	mu-soo-bi da-she	open stance
nekoashi dachi	nee-ko-a-she da-she	cat stance
nigiri game	nigilli gammay	weighted jars
nihon nukite	nee-hon nook-ettay	split spear hand
nogare	no-gorray	long and short wave breathing
nunchaku	nun-chak-oo	rice flail
nukite	nook-ettay	spear hand or straight finger thrust
nukite jodan uchi	nook-ettay jaw-dan oo-chi	spear hand upper strike
rei	r-lay	bow
renshi	r-len-she	instructor of high attainment
sai	sigh	truncheon
sambon kumite	sam-bon kum-ettay	three-step pre-arranged sparring
samurai	sam-oo-lie	Japanese knight or warrior
sanchin dachi	san-shin da-she	diamond stance
seiki juku	say-key jew-koo	true spirit school
seiken	say-ken	striking fist with first two knuckles
seiza	say-za	seated posture
sensei	sen-say	teacher, or he who has gone before
shihan	she-han	Karate Master
shiko dachi	she-ko da-she	sumo stance
shita tsuki	sh-ta ski	inverted punch
shizen tai	she-zen tie	natural stance
shotei	sho-tay	palm heel
shotei gedan uke	sho-tay gee-dan oo-kay	palm heel lower block
shotei jodan uke	sho-tay jaw-dan oo-kay	palm heel upper block
shotei uchi	sho-tay oo-chi	palm heel strike
shotei morote uchi	sho-tay mo-rot-ay oo-chi	palm heel double strike
shuto gedan barai	shtol gee-dan bal-eye	knife hand lower parry

shuto mawashi uke	shtol ma-washee oo-kay	knife hand roundhouse block
shuto sokotsu uchi	shtol so-kottsu oo-chi	knife hand strike to collar bone
shuto yoko ganmen uchi	shtol yok-ow gan-men oo-chi	knife hand strike to head
shuto yoki uchi	shtol yok-ow oo-chi	side knife hand strike
sokuto	sock-oo-toe	knife foot
soto uke	sotto-oo-kay	outside block
taisabaki	tie-sa-ba-kee	body management
tameshiwari	tammi-she-a-wa-ee	test of destruction, breaking of solid objects
te	tay	hand
teisoku	tay-sock-oo	sole of foot
tettsui	tet-soo-i	hammer fist
tettsui jodan uchi	tet-soo-i jaw-dan oo-chi	hammer fist upper strike
tsuriashi dachi	t-soori-a-she da-she	crane stance
tobi ushiro geri	to-be oo-shillo gelli	jumping back kick
todei	toe-day	Chinese hand
toho	toe-ho	sword hand
tou	t-ow	cane bundle
tonfa	tonn-fa	rice grinder
uchi	oo-chi	strike
uchi hachiji dachi	oo-chi ha-jiji da-she	pigeon-toe stance
uchi uke	oo-chi oo-kay	inside block
uke	oo-kay	block
ushiro geri	u-she-lo gelli	back kick
ushiro mawashi geri	u-she-lo ma-washee gelli	rear roundhouse kick
uraken	yule-aken	back fist
uraken hizo uchi	yule-aken he-zo oo-chi	spleen strike
uraken yoko uchi	yule-aken yok-ow oo-chi	side back fist strike
uraken shomen uchi	yule-aken sho-men oo-chi	back fist face strike
yakusoku kumite	yako-sock-o kum-ettay	pre-arranged sparring
yang	y-ang	positive
ying	y-ing	negative
yoi dachi	yoy da-she	prepared stance
yoko geri sokuto	yok-ow gelli sock-oo-toe	side kick
yon-ju-go kakato geri	yon-jew-go ka-ka-toe gelli	45° heel kick
zazen	za-zen	controlled breathing exercises whilst in seiza
zenkutsu dachi	zen-kut-soo da-she	forward leaning stance